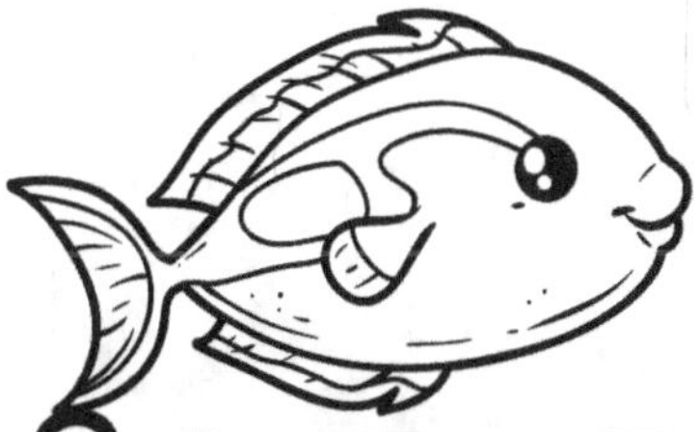

JUST KEEP COLORING!

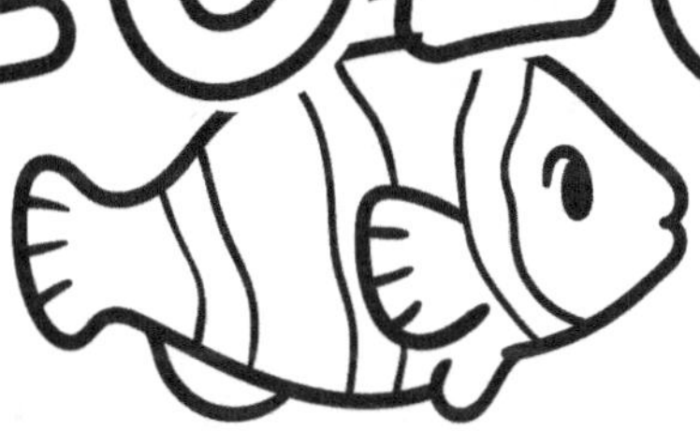

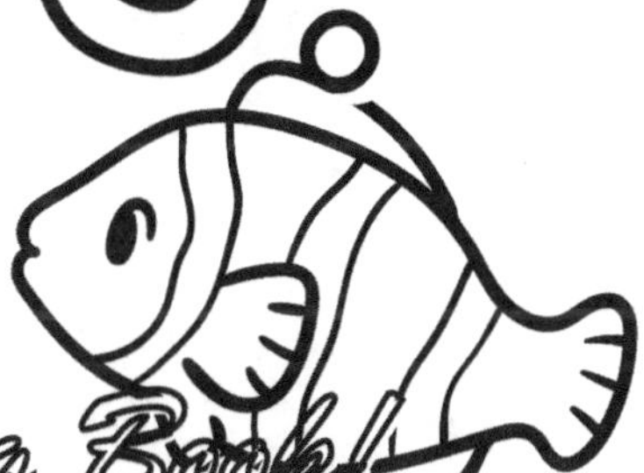

A Fin-tasticly Fishy Coloring Book!

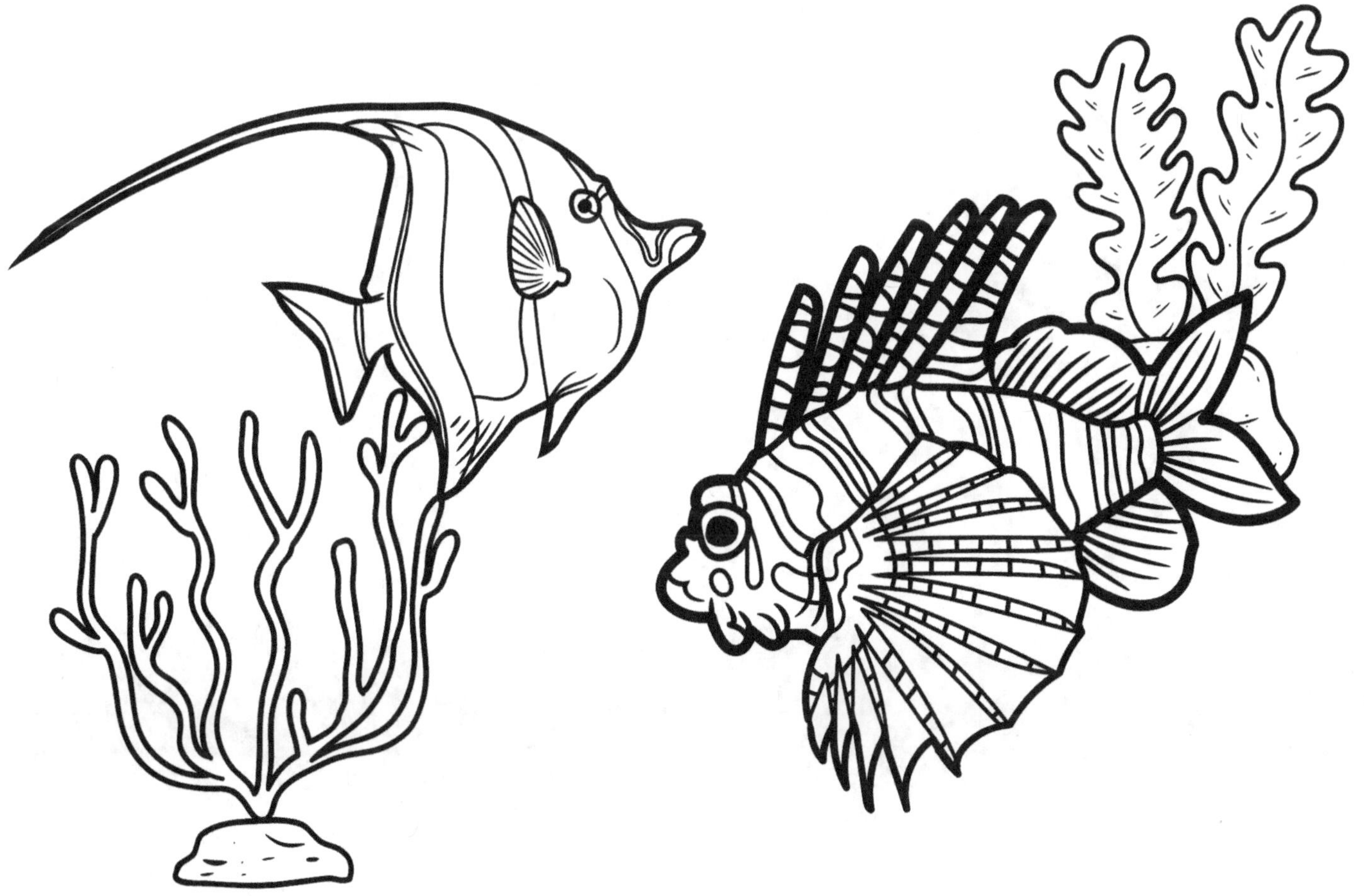

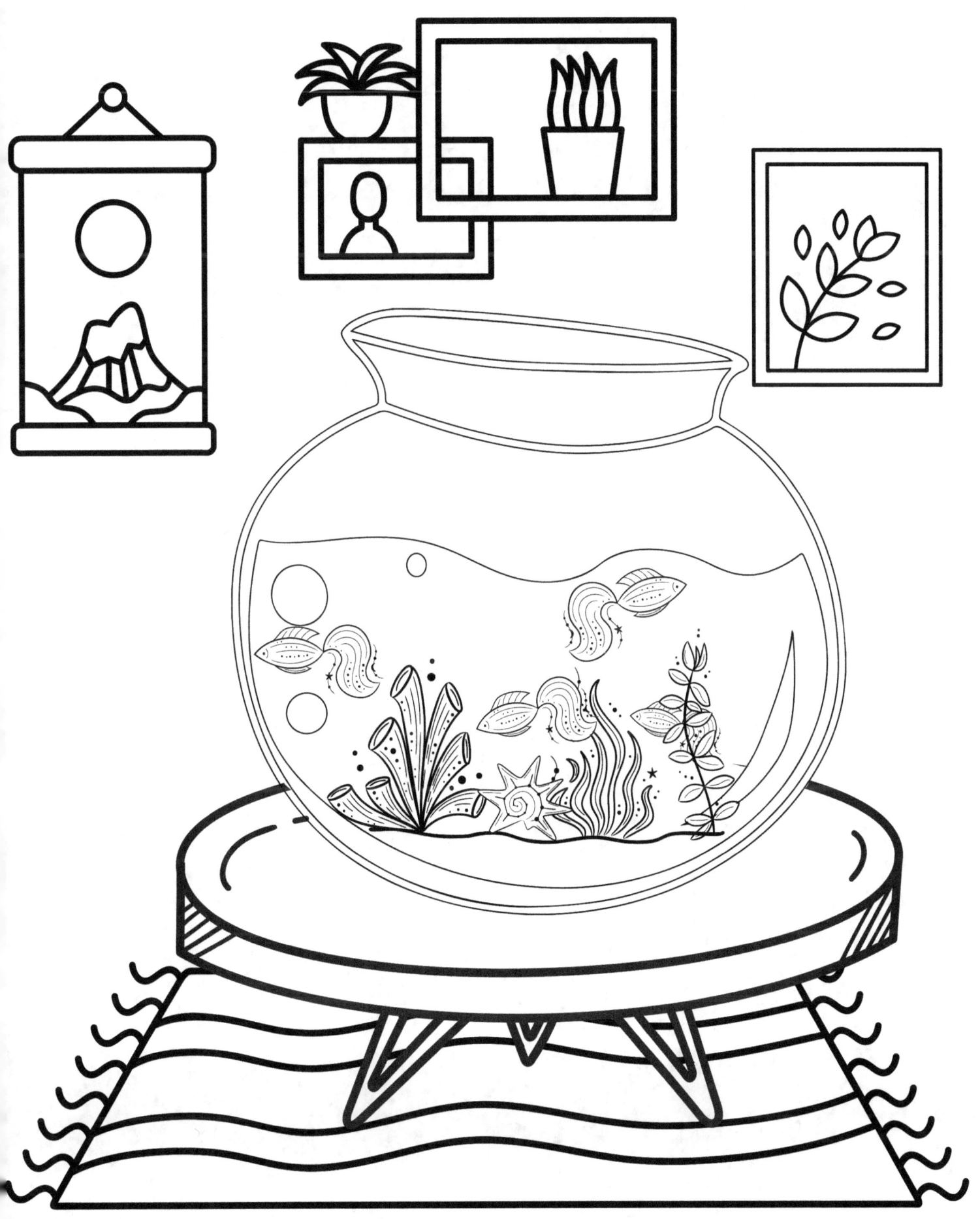

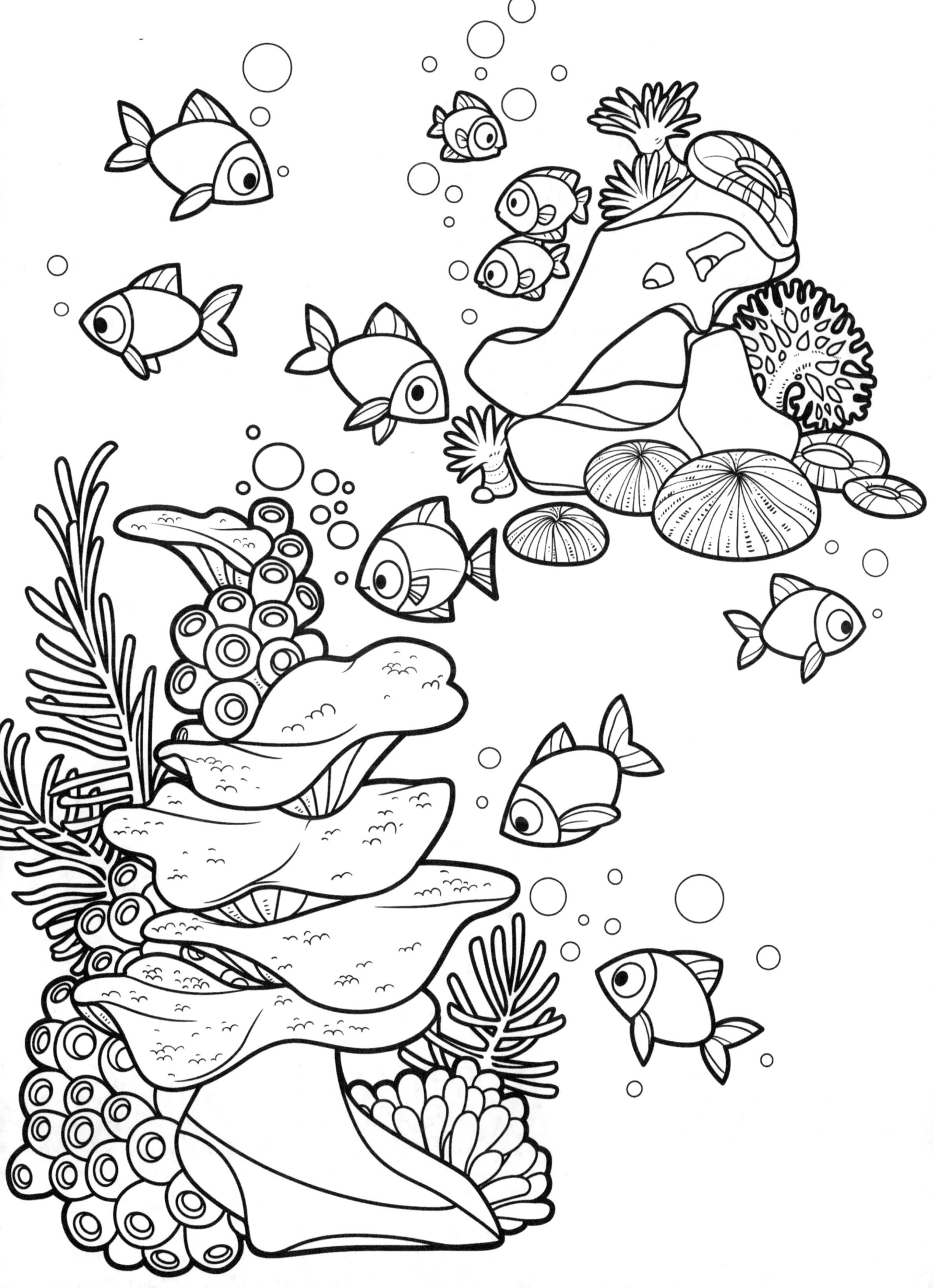

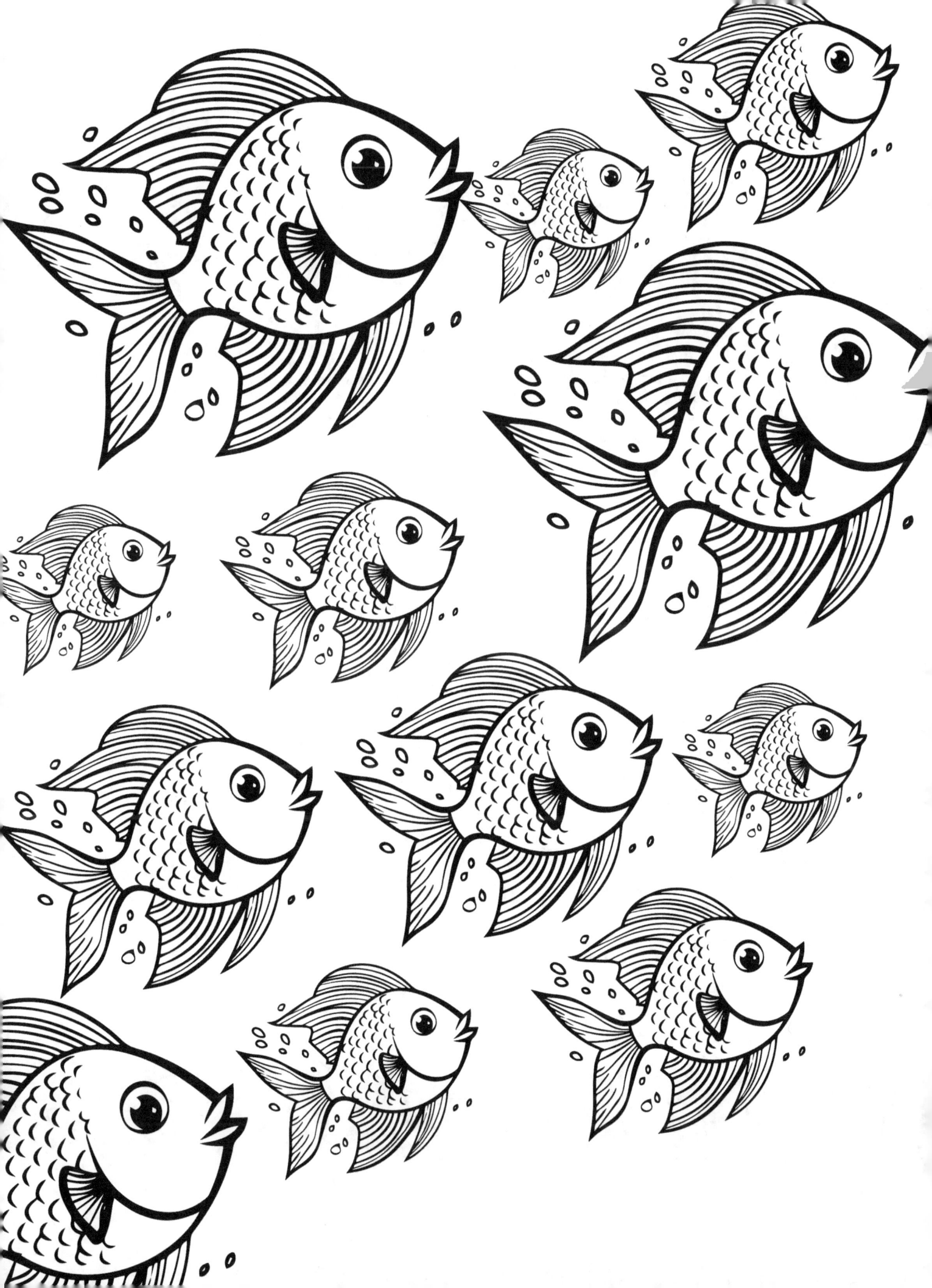

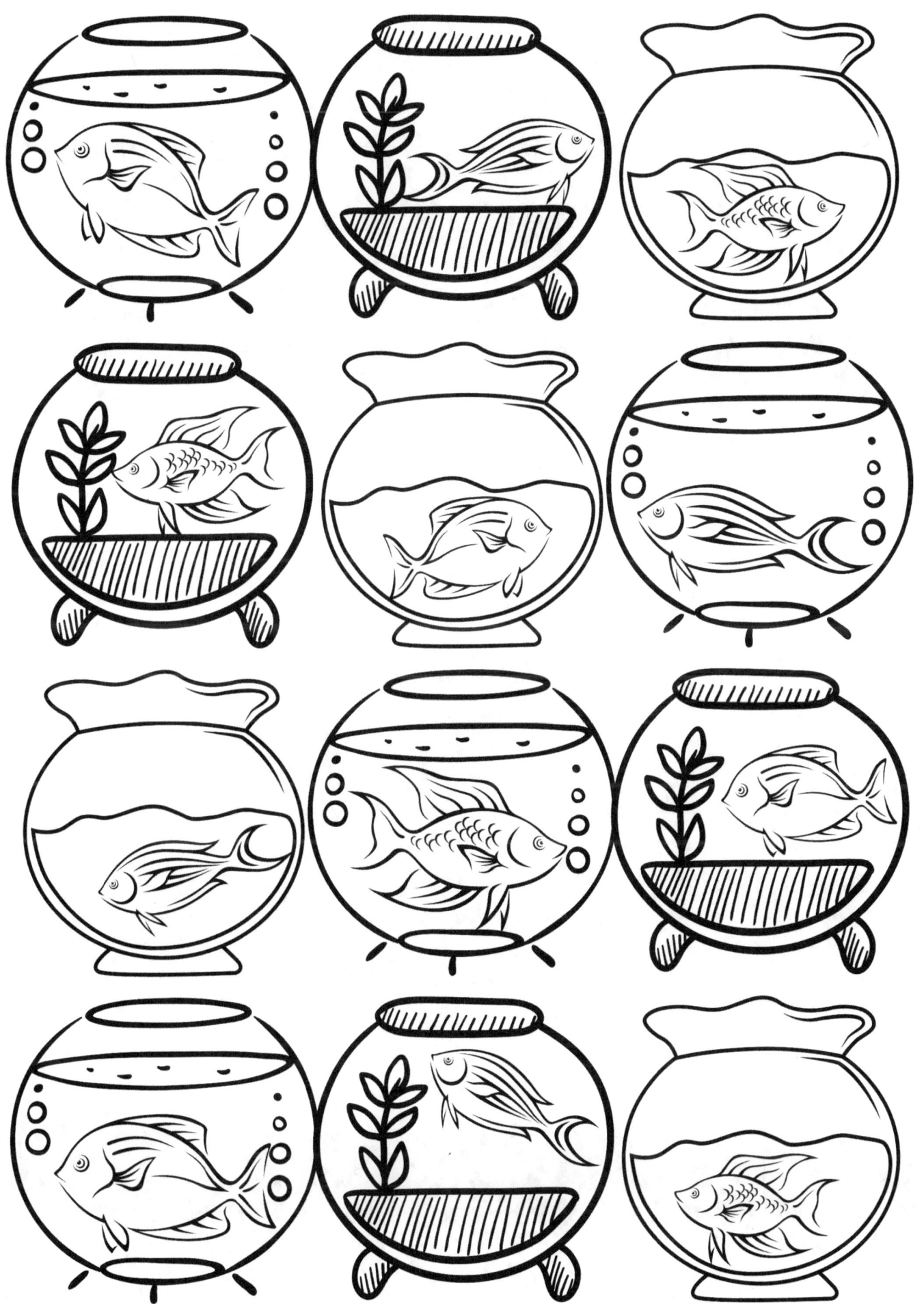

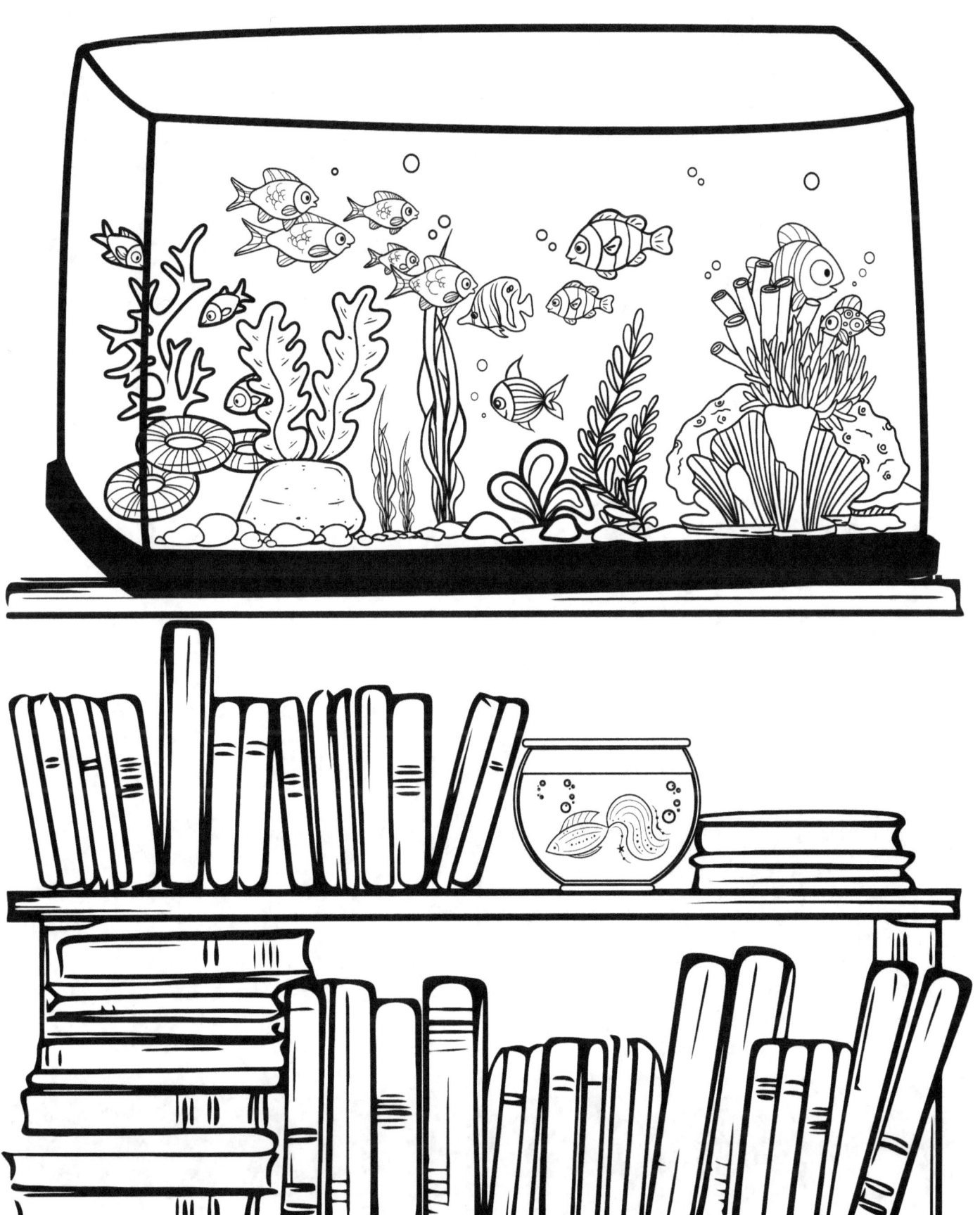

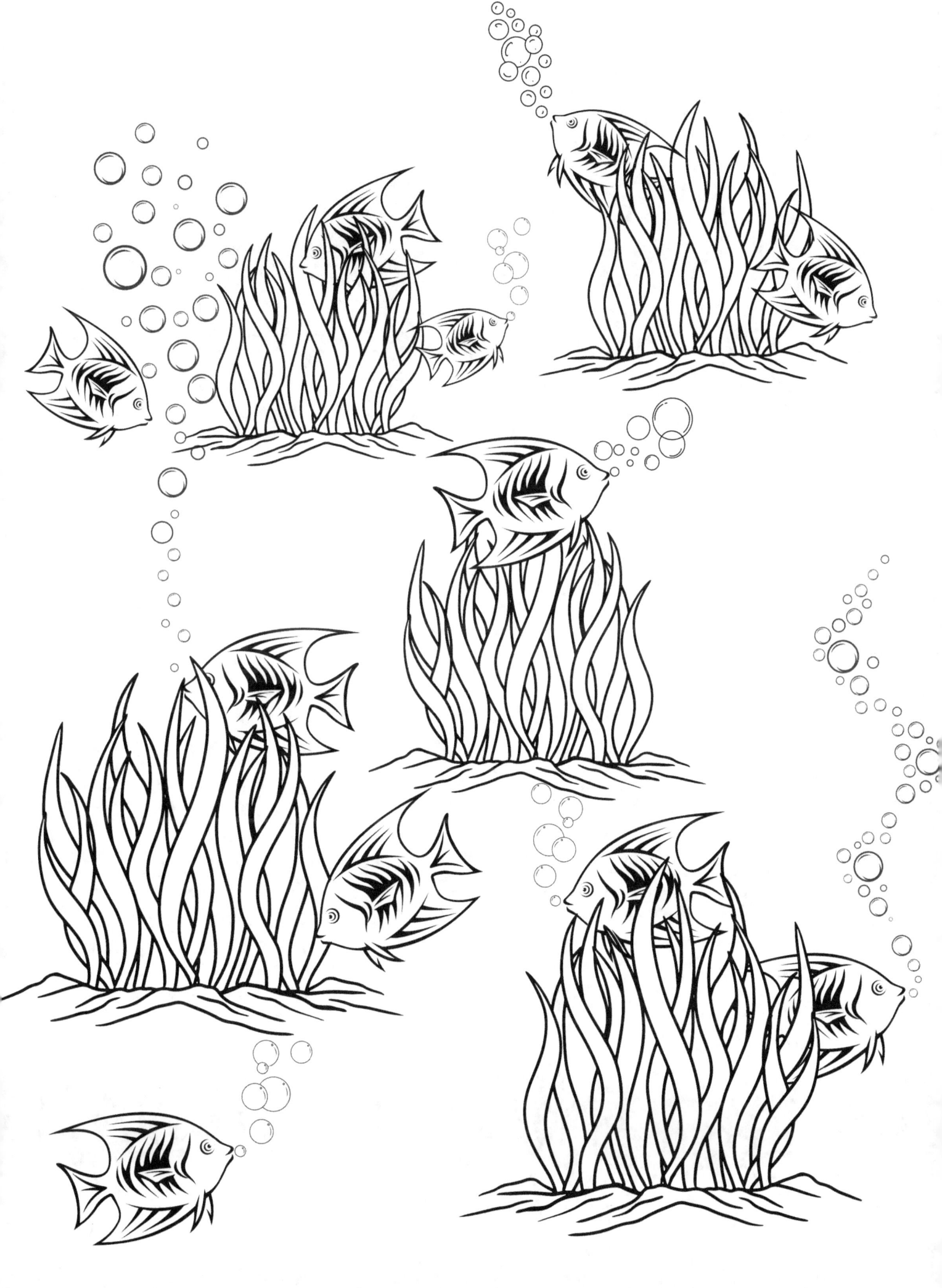

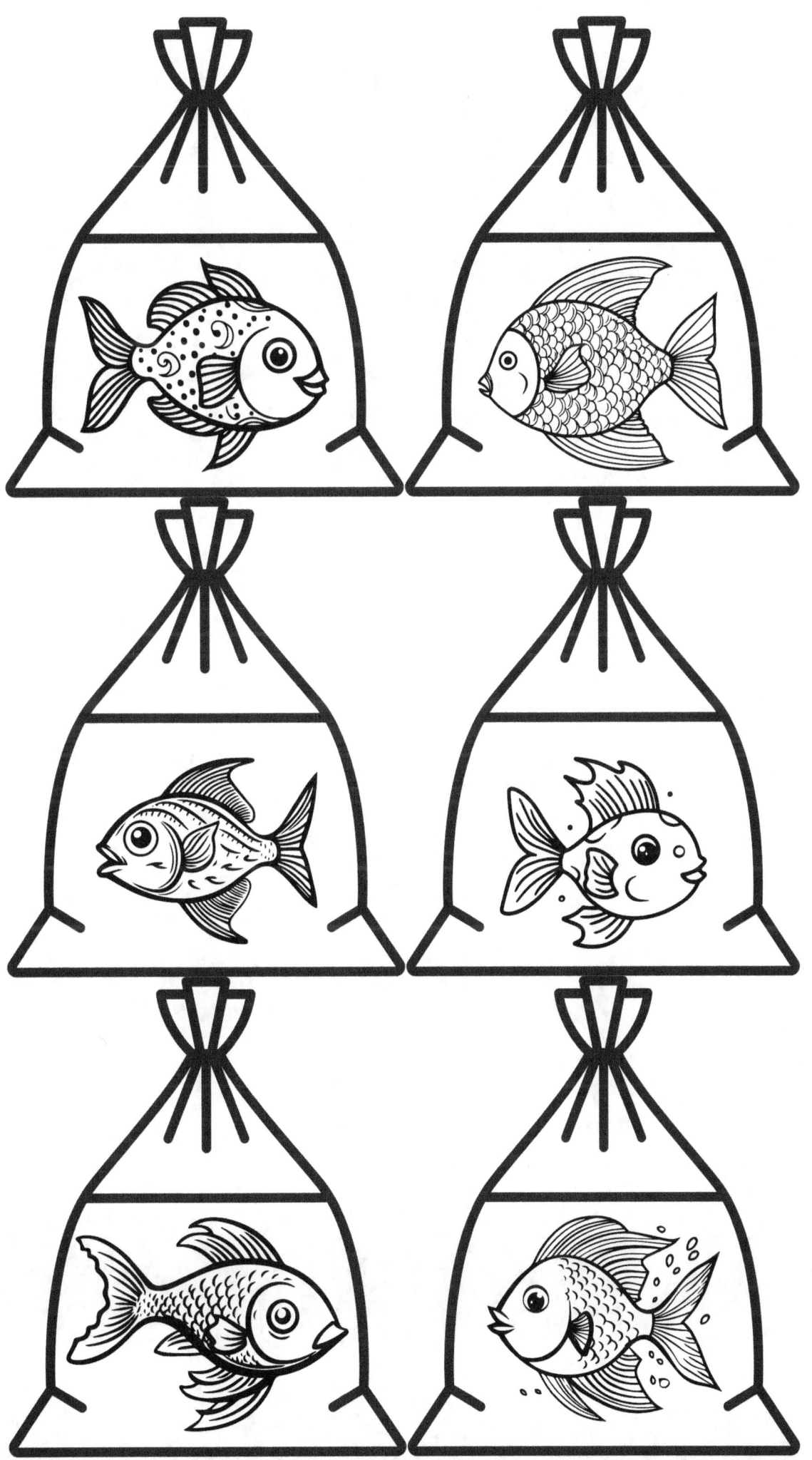

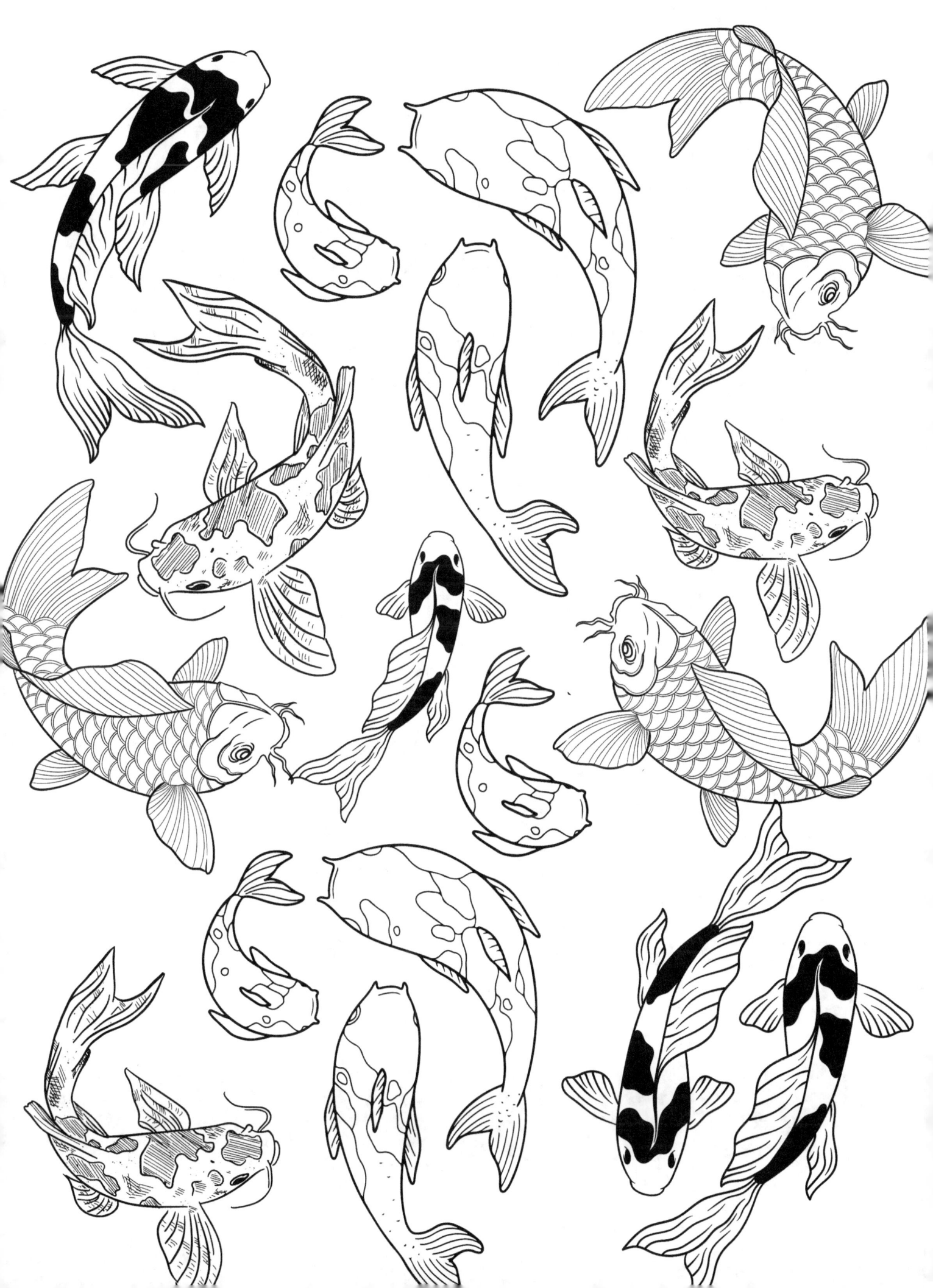

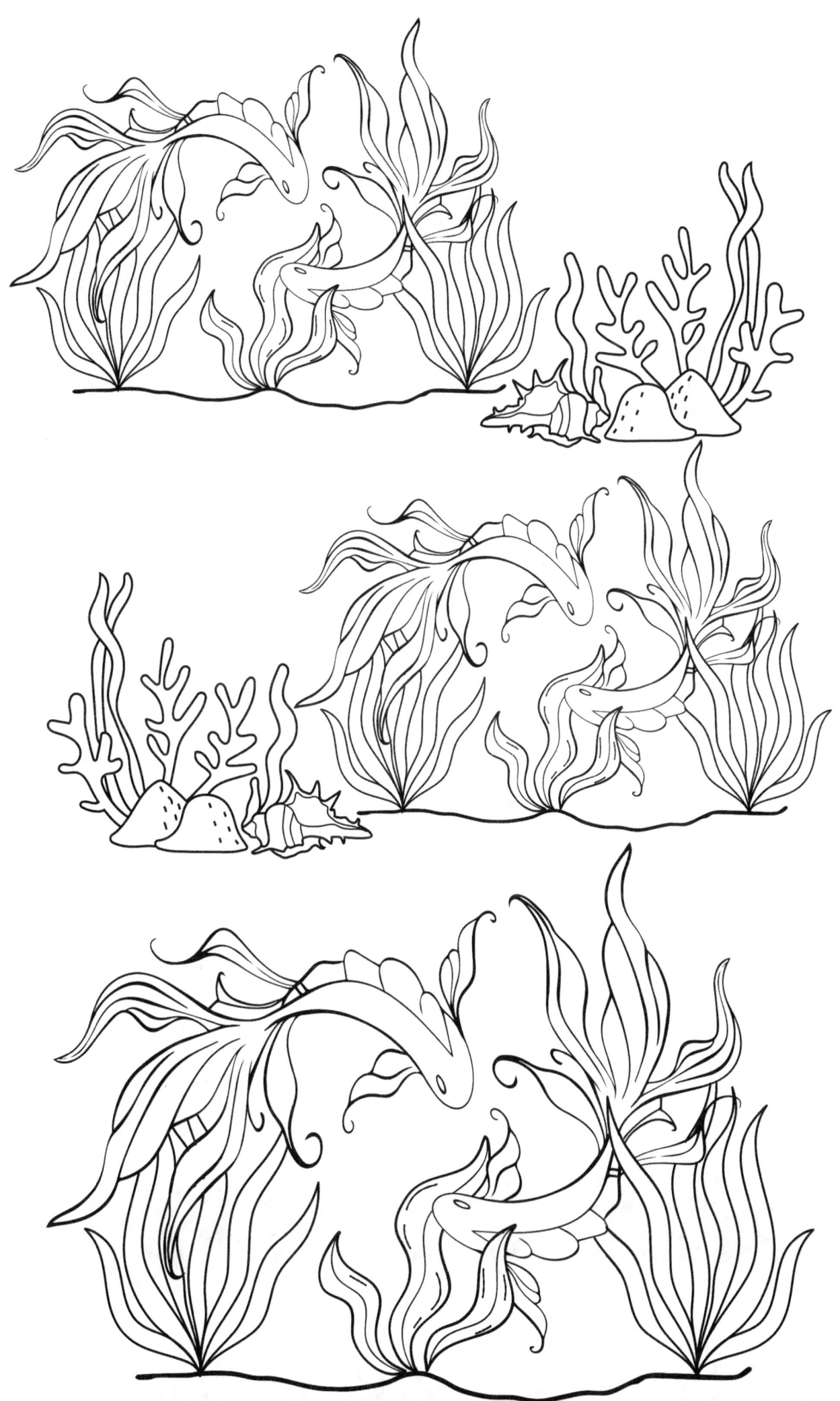

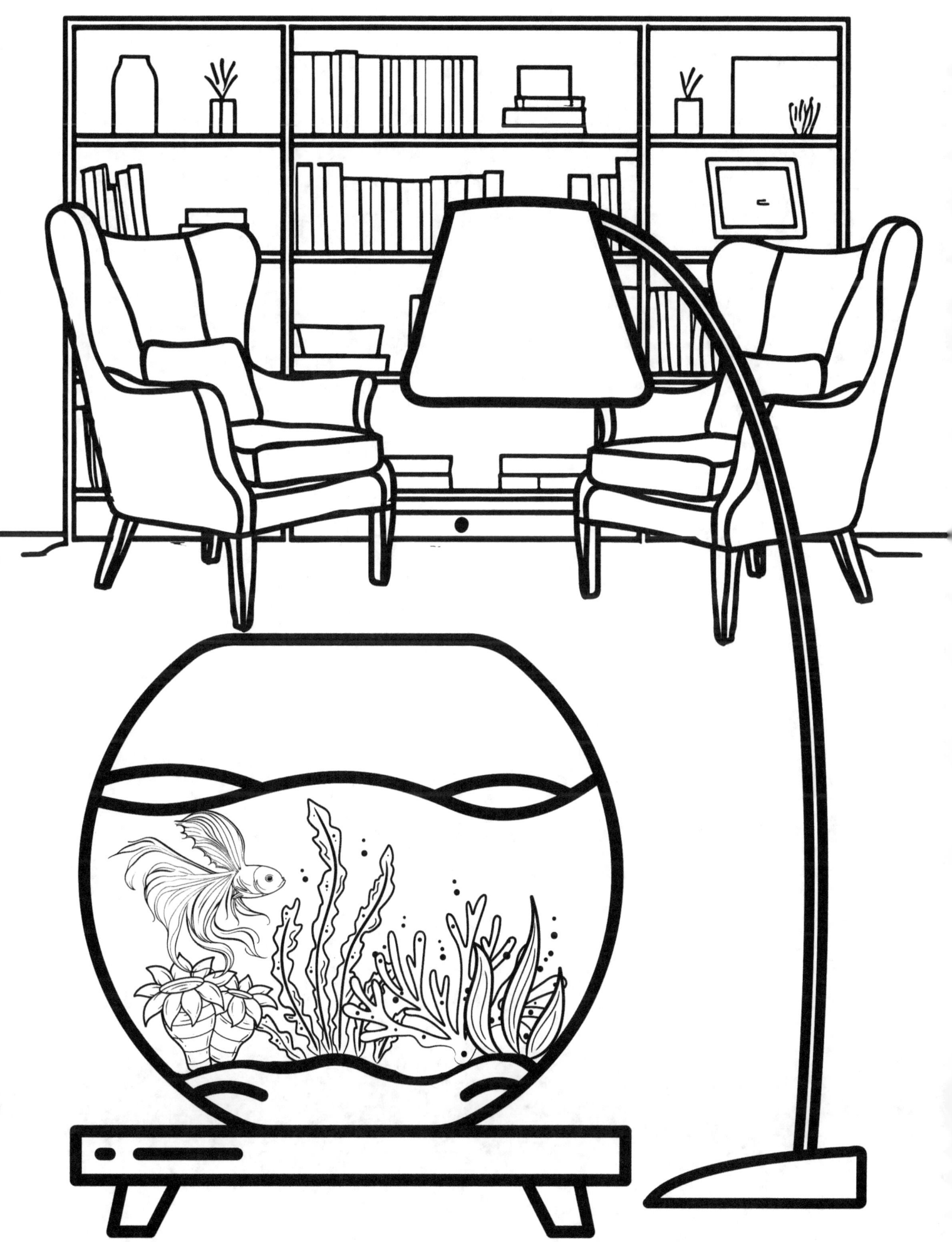

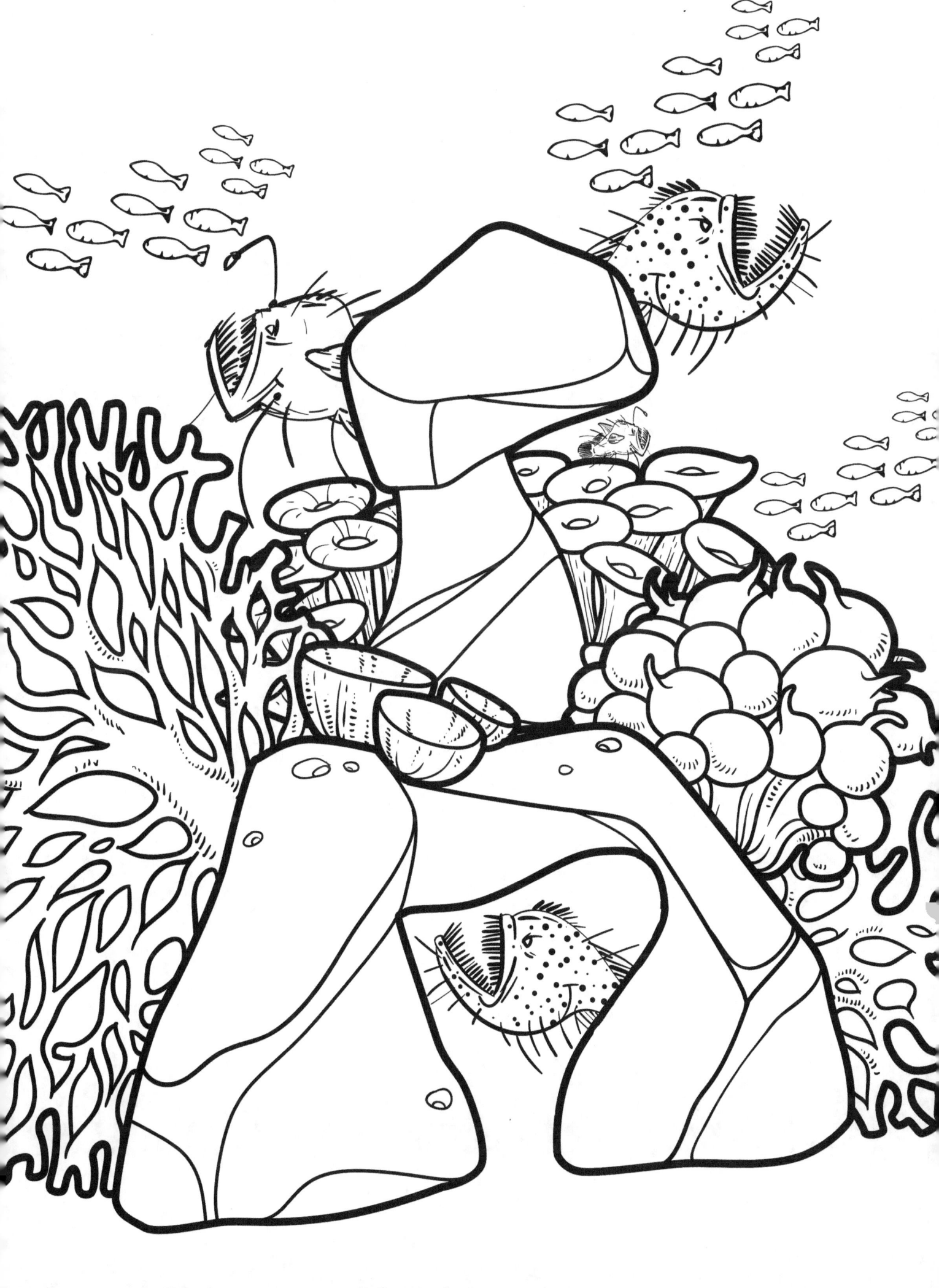

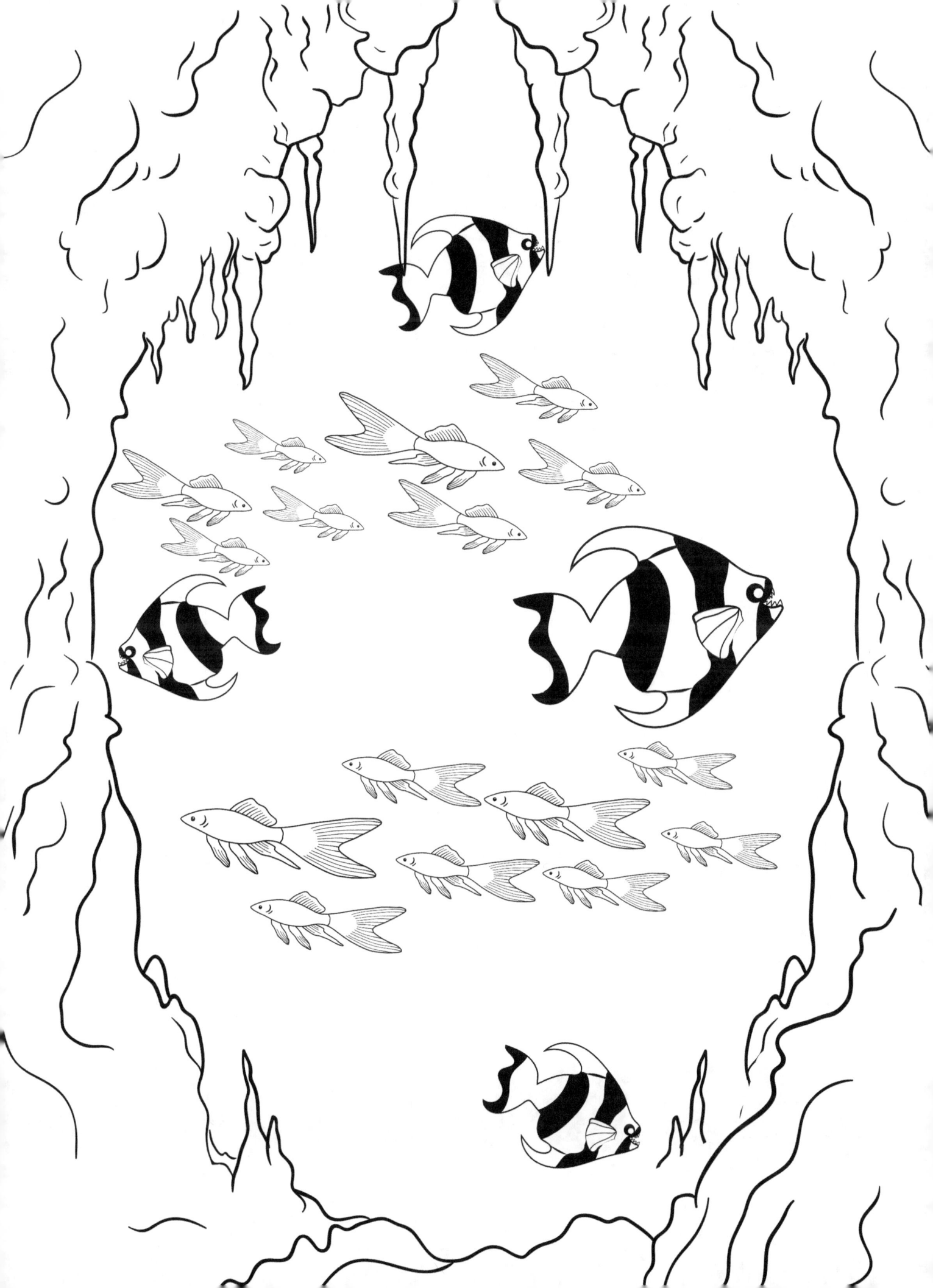

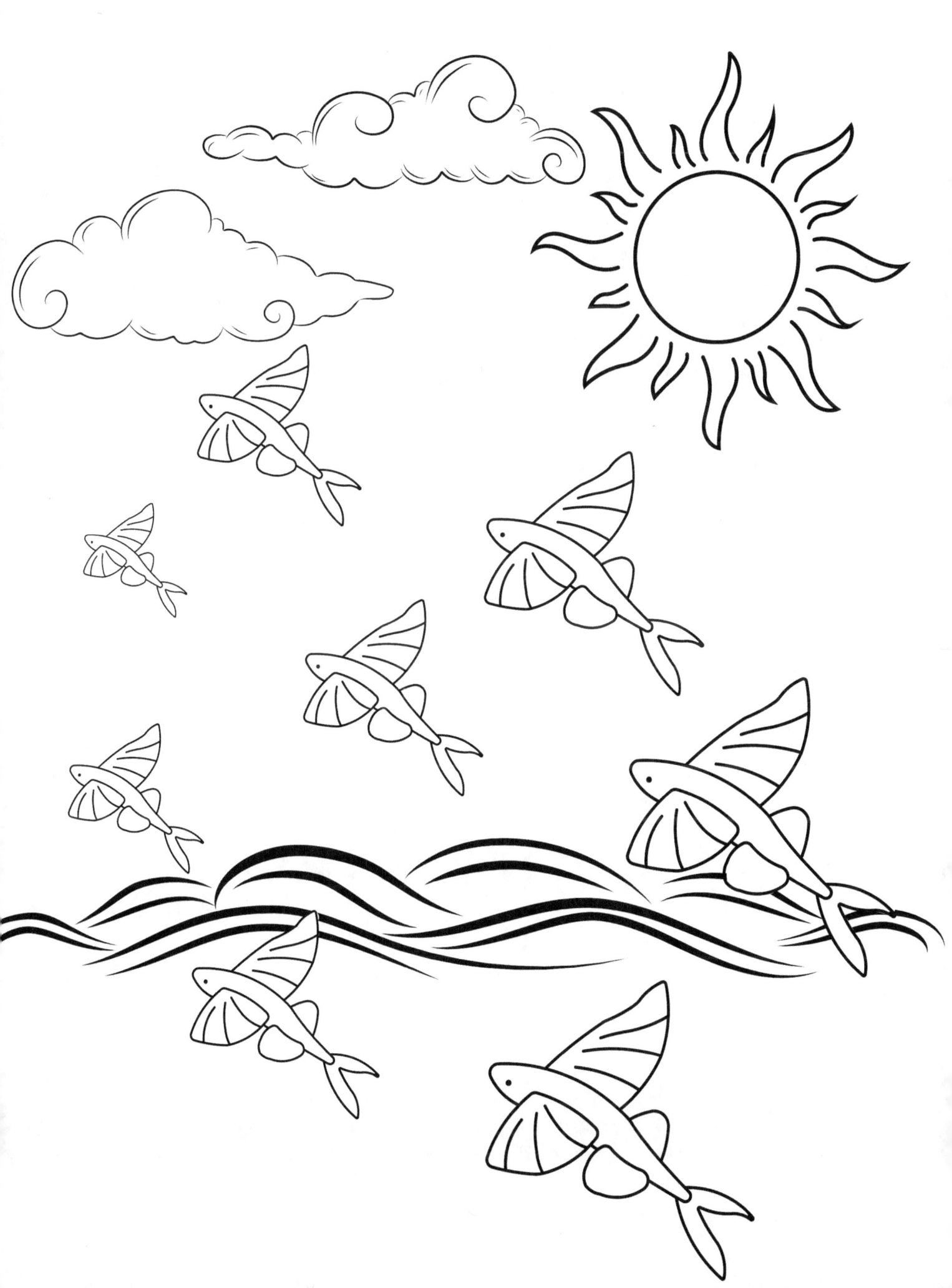

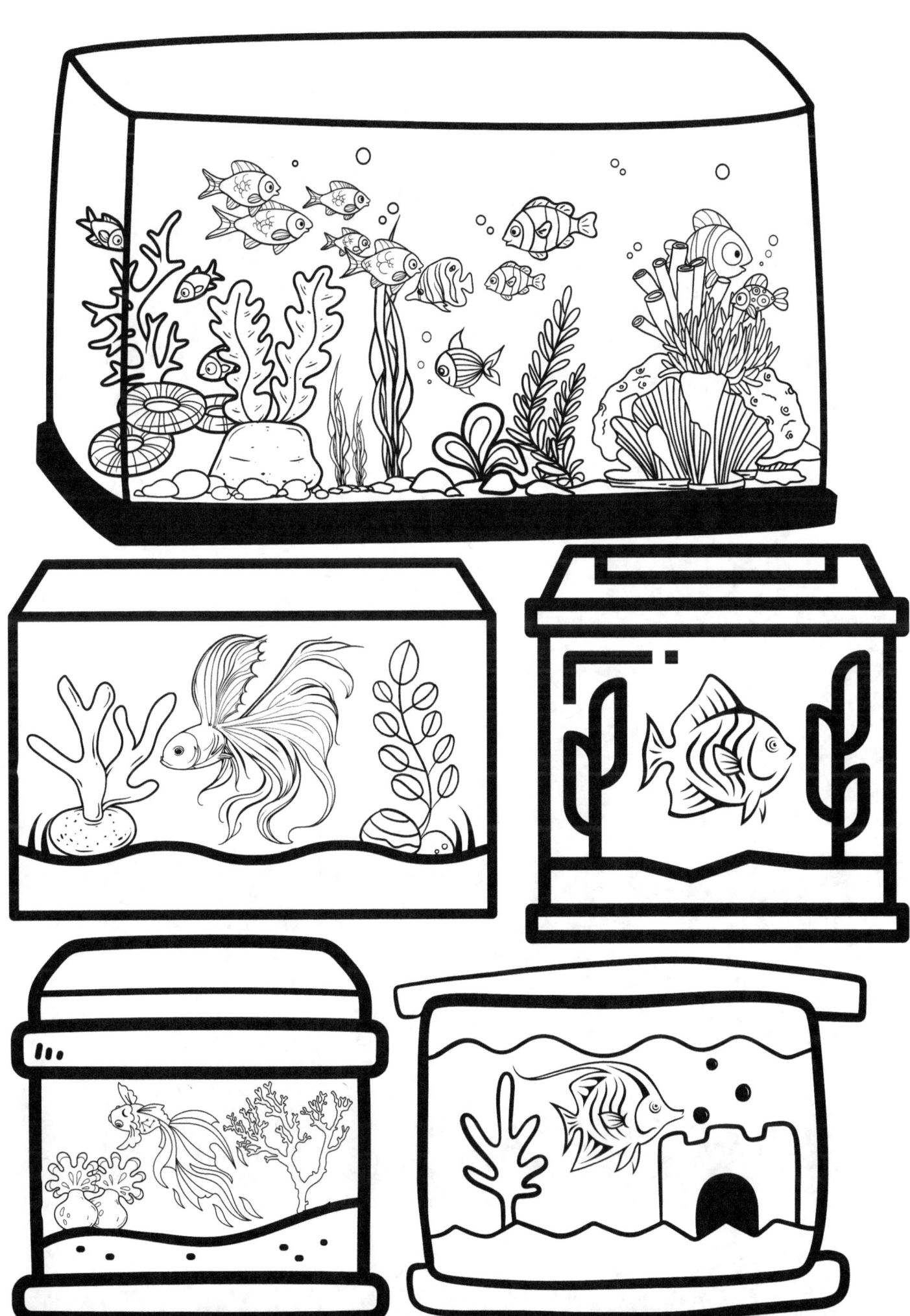

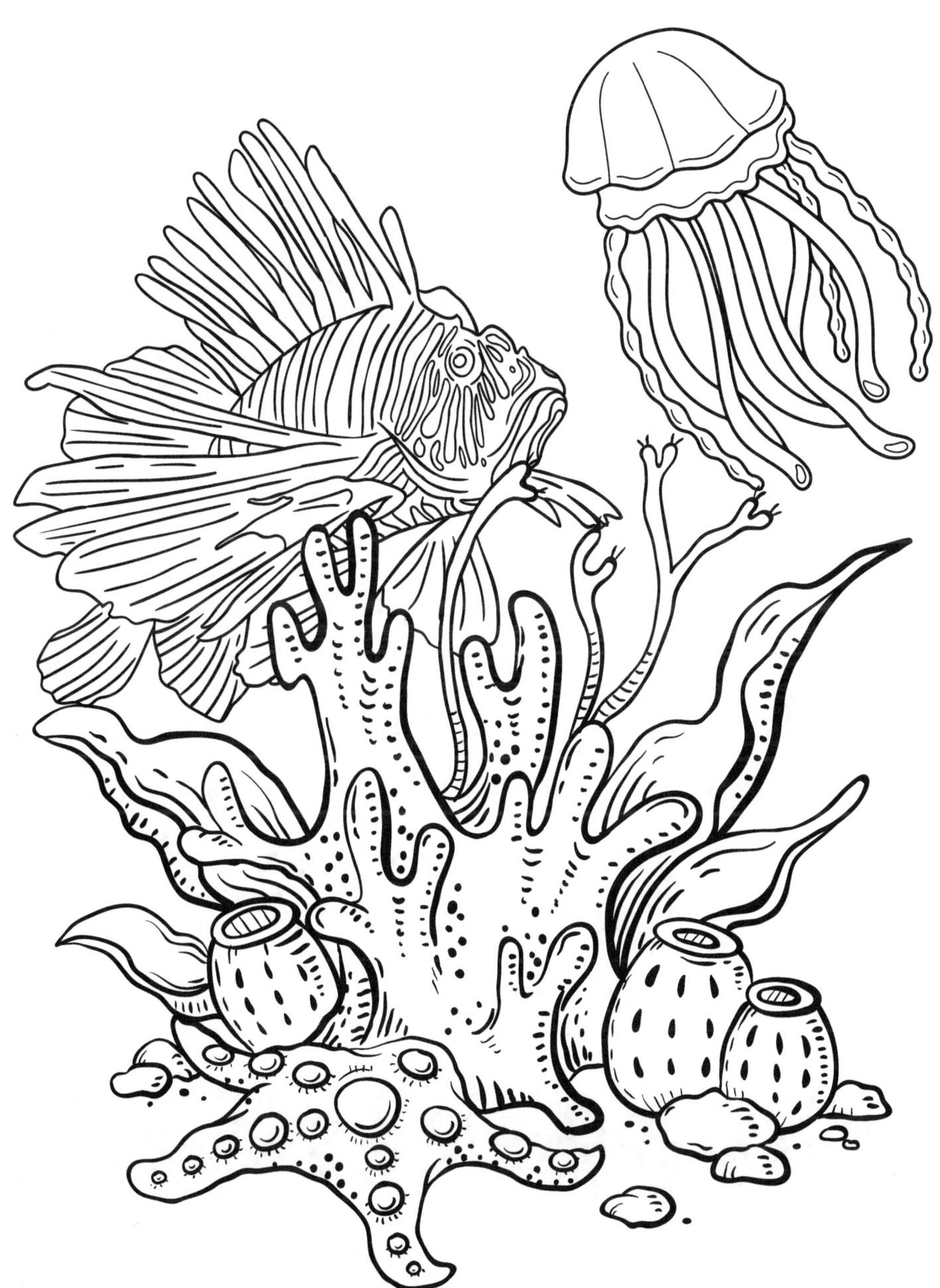

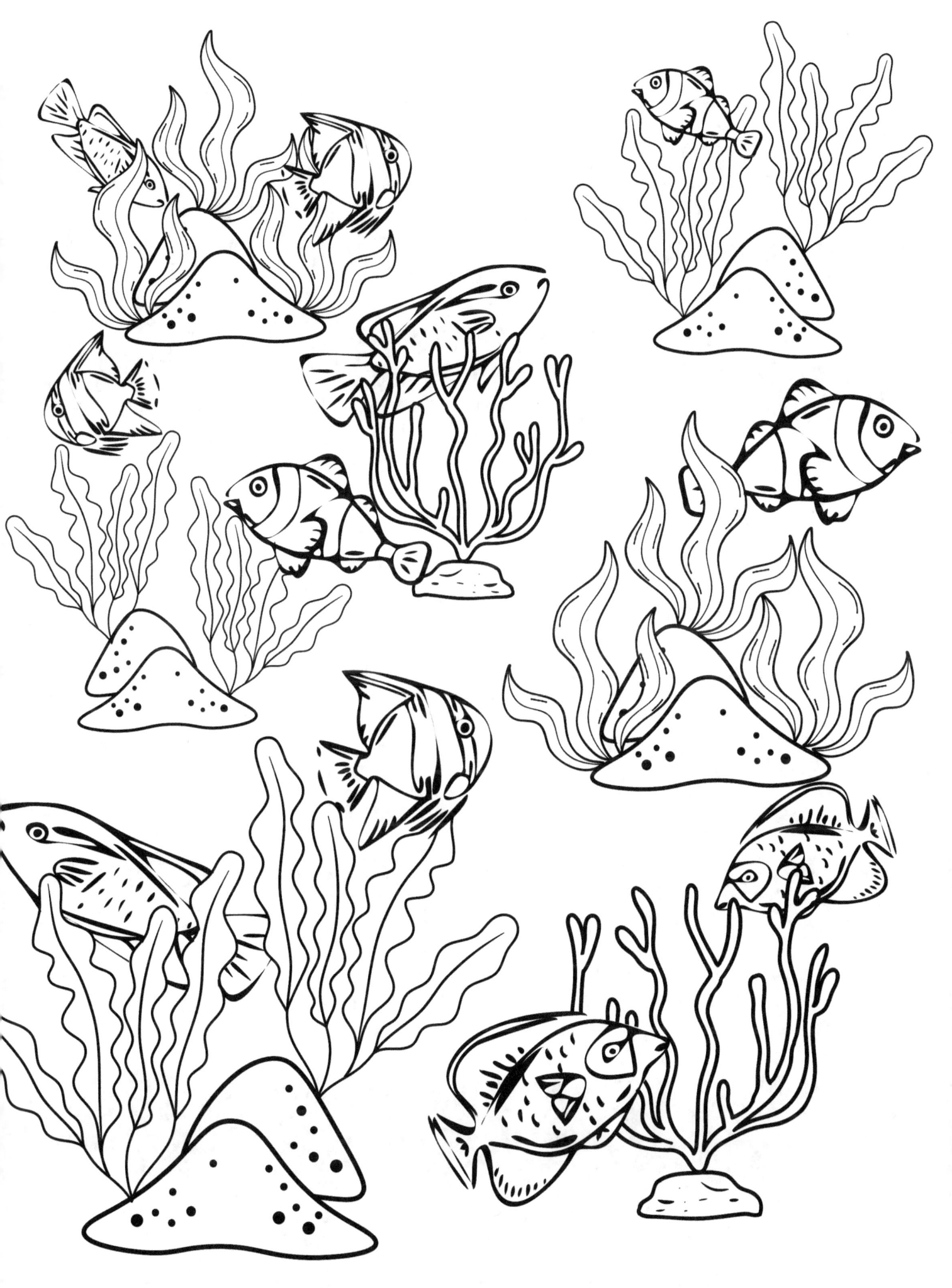

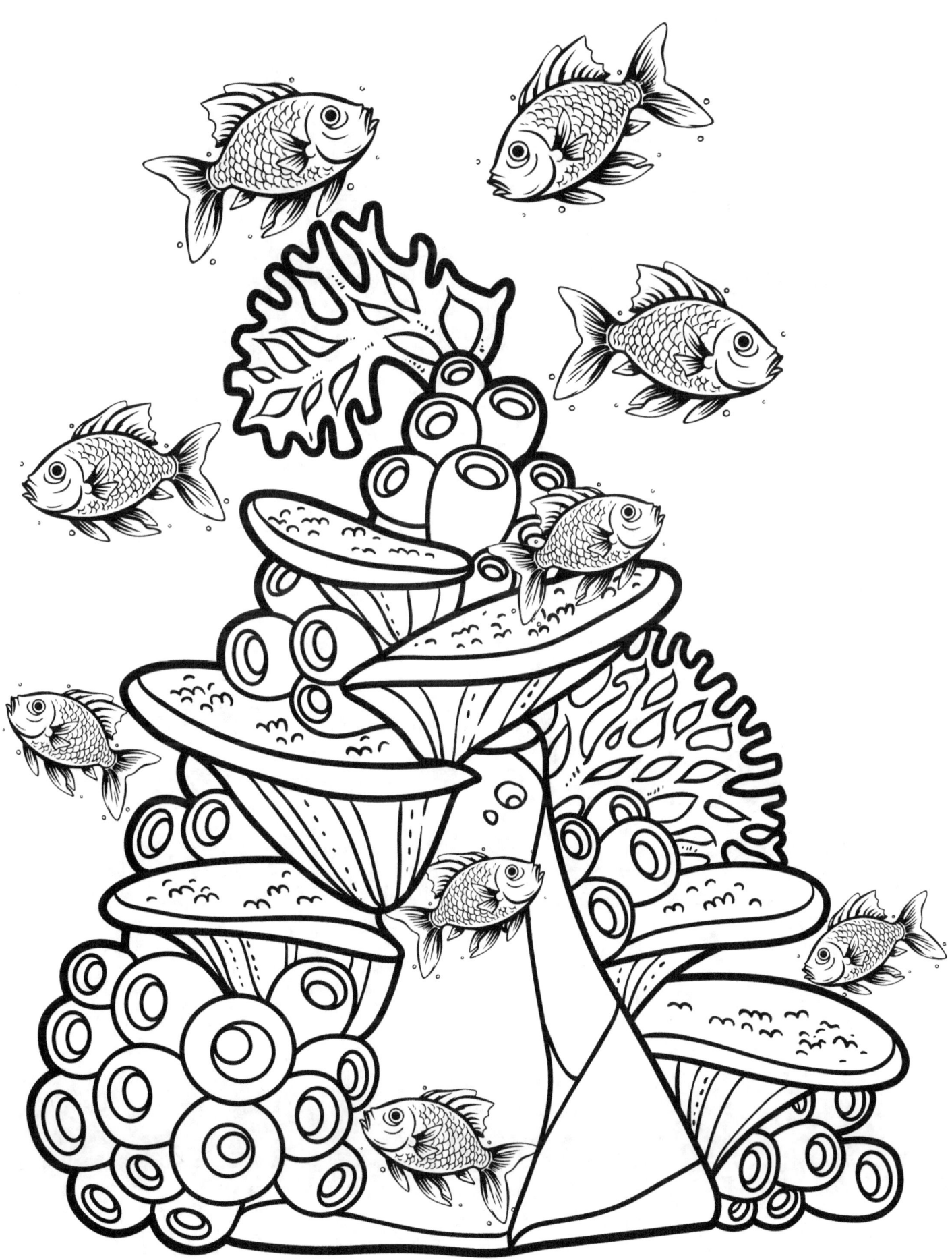

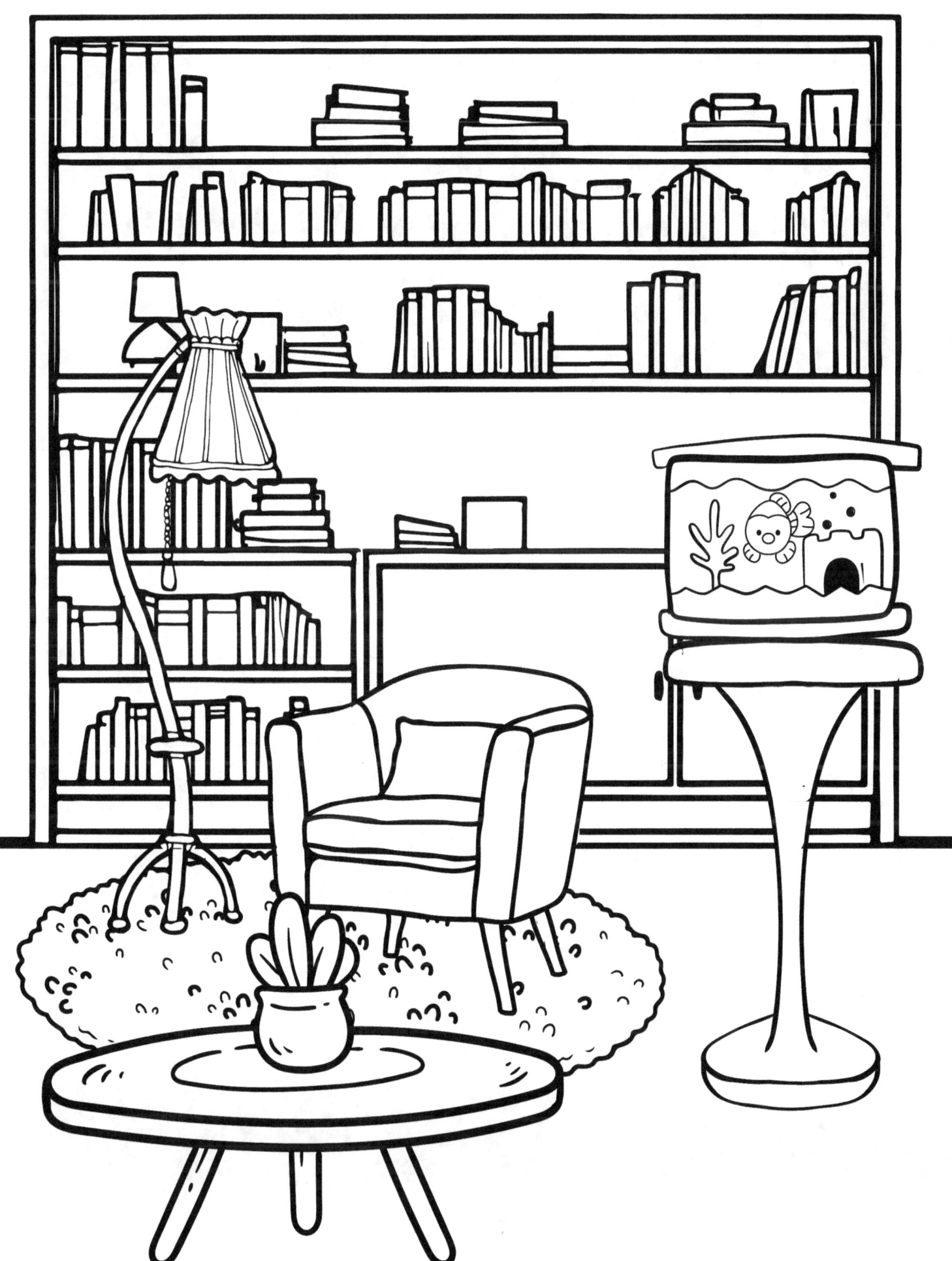

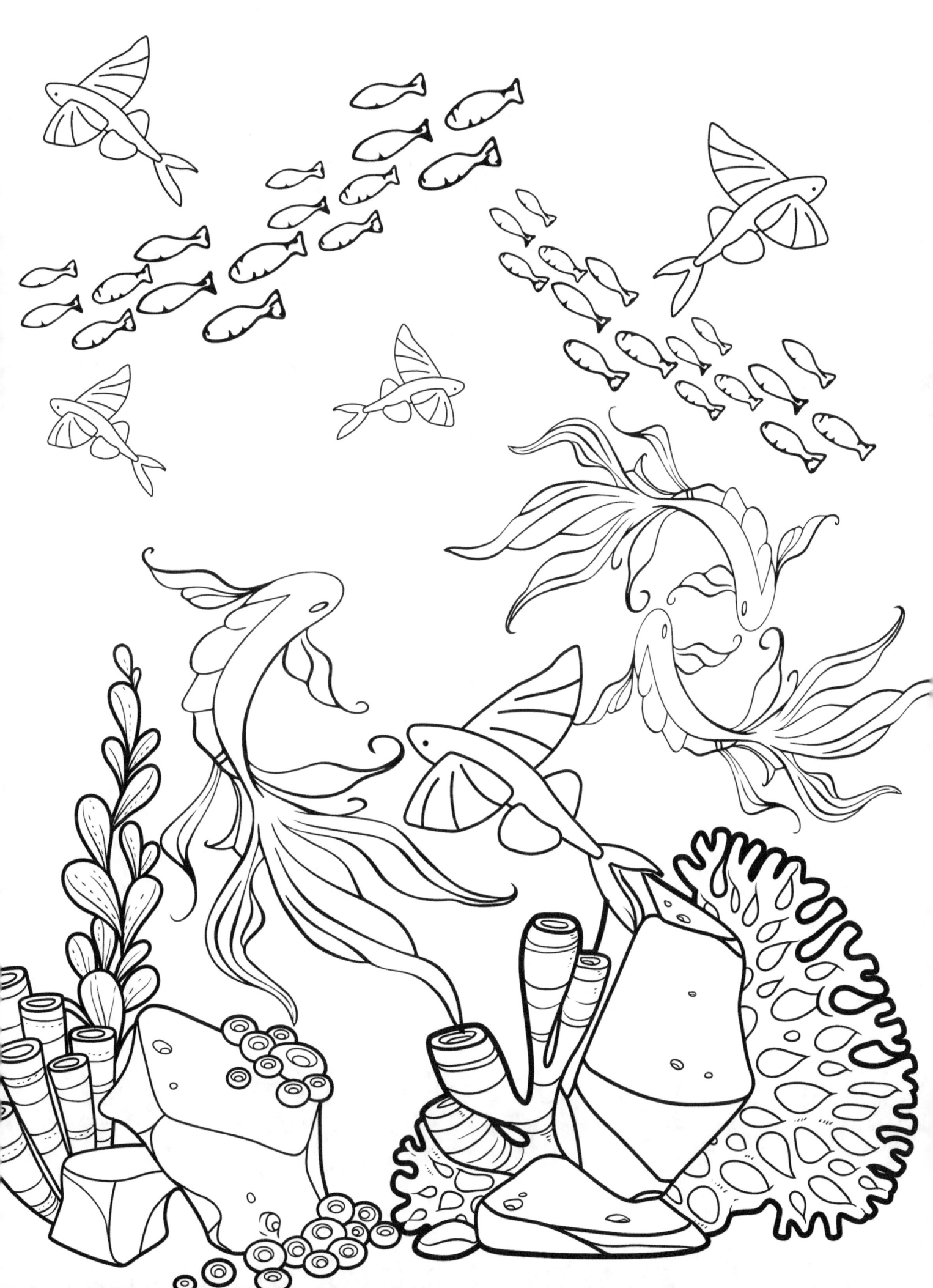

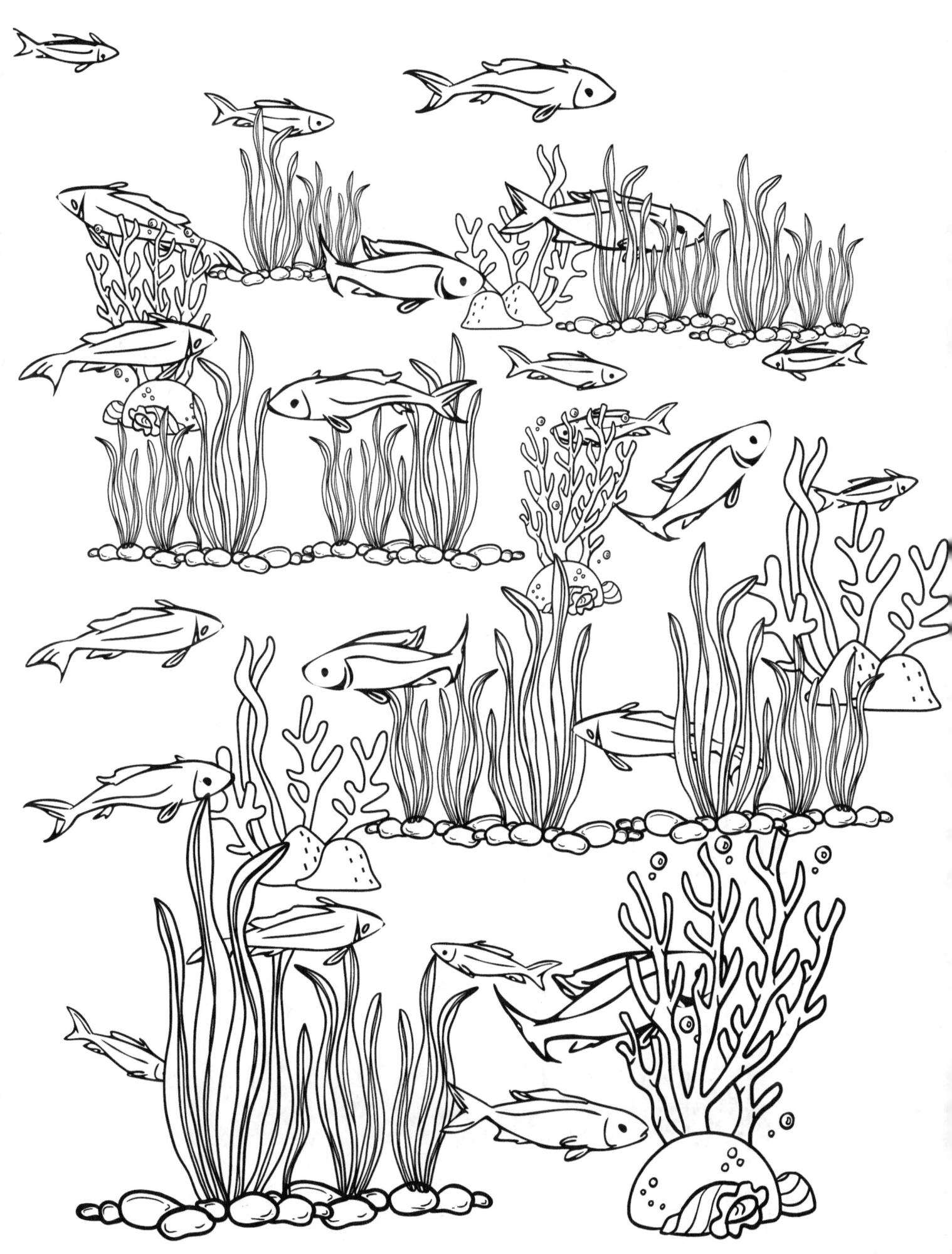

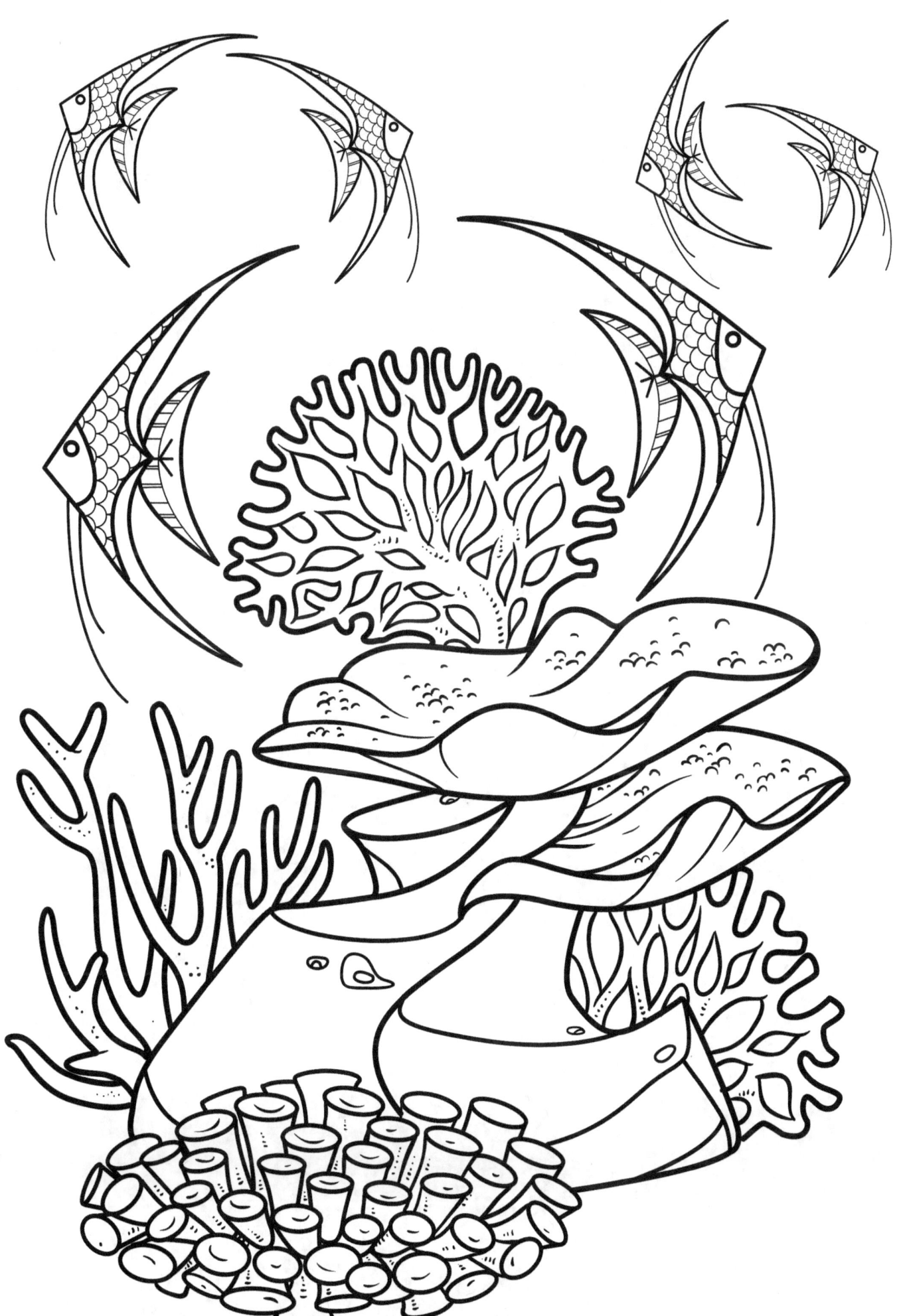

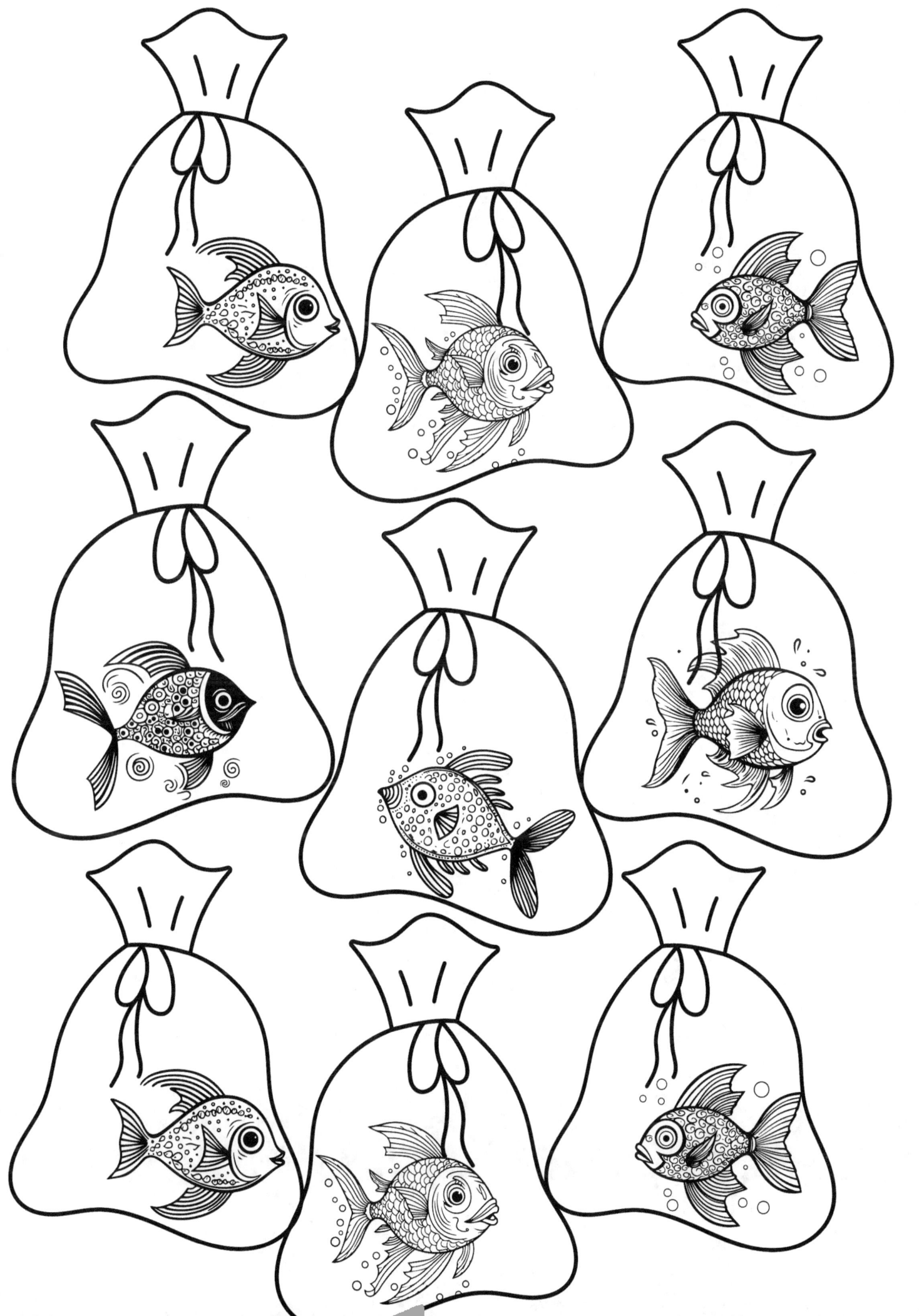

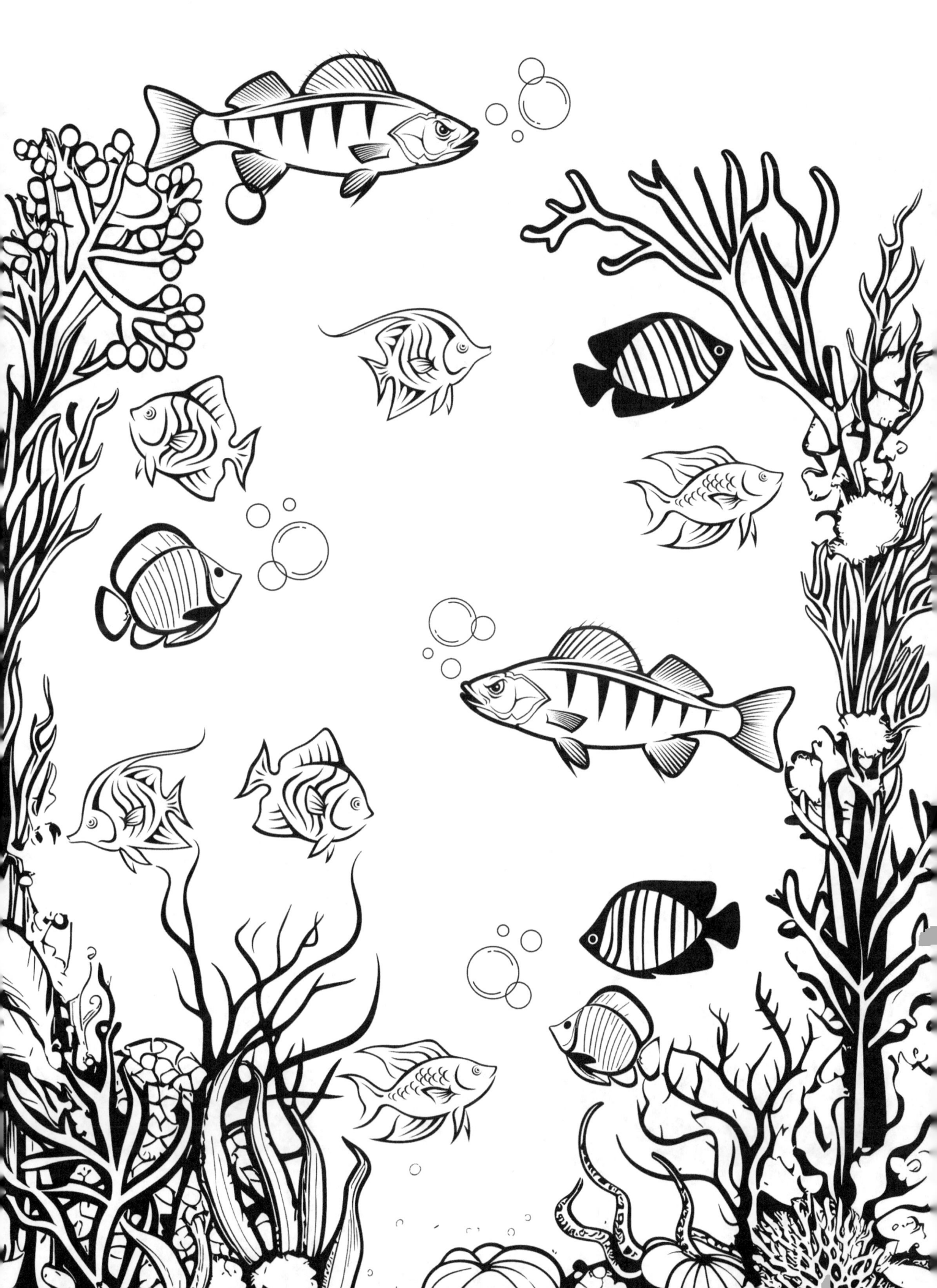

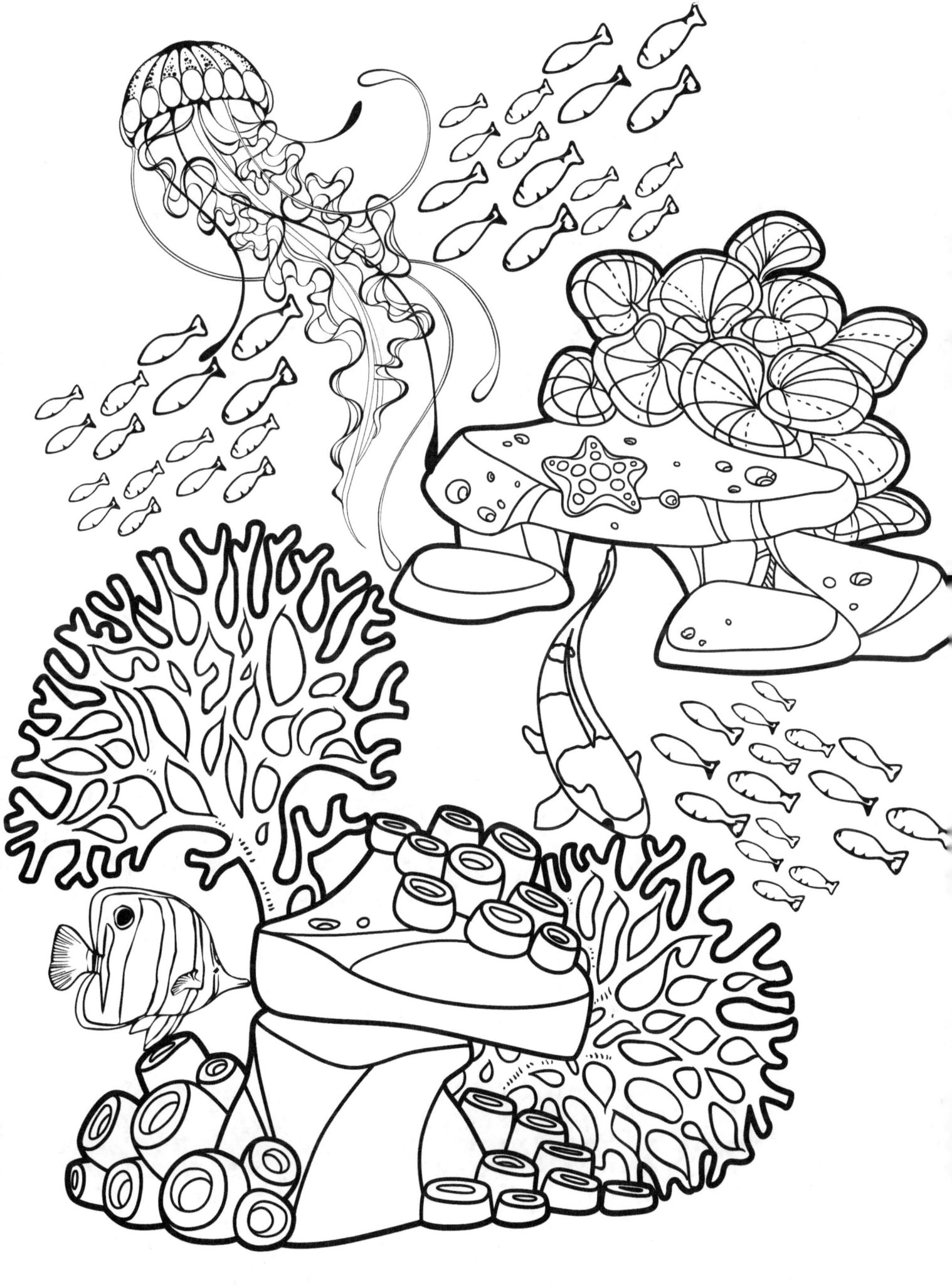

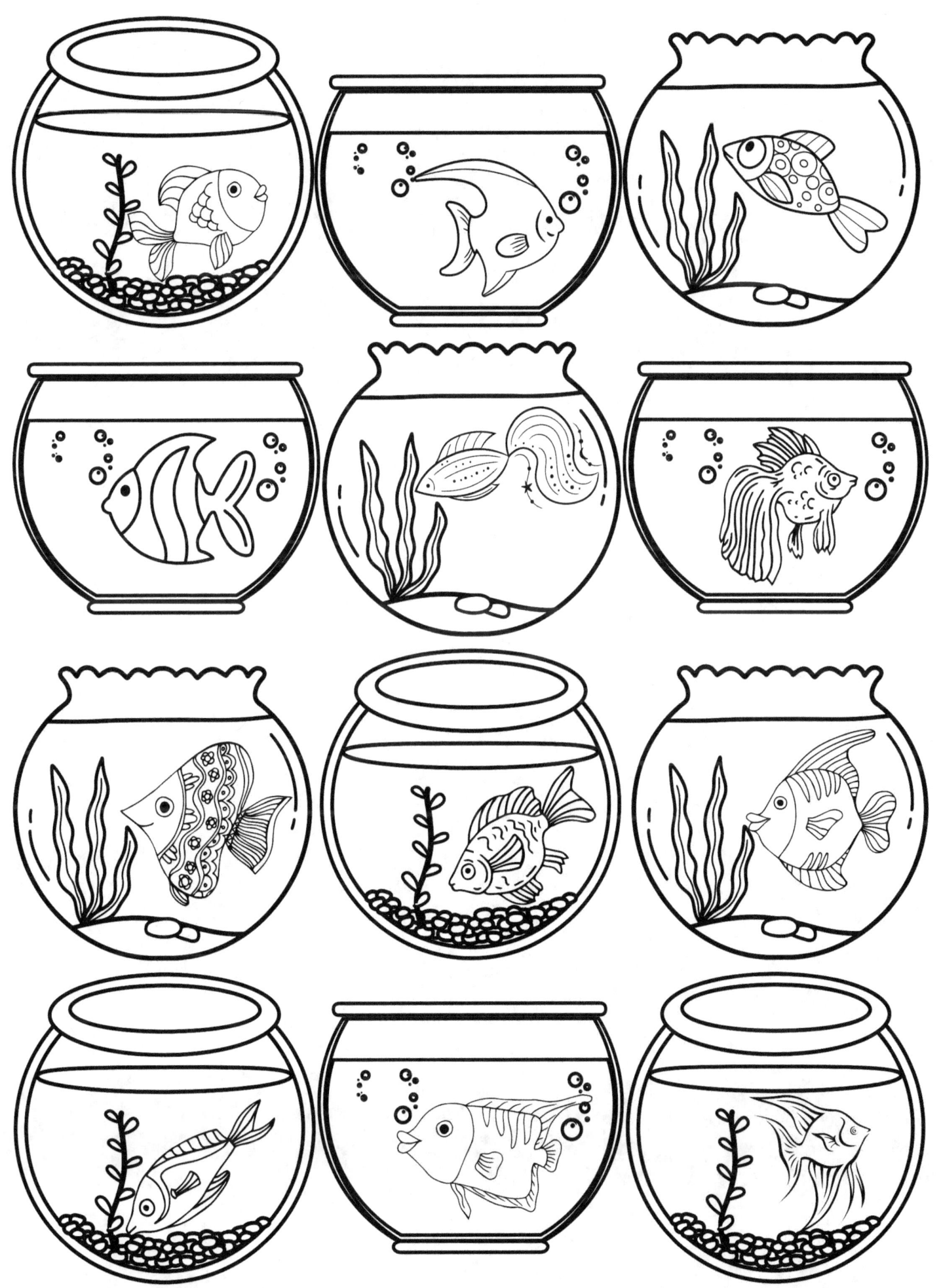

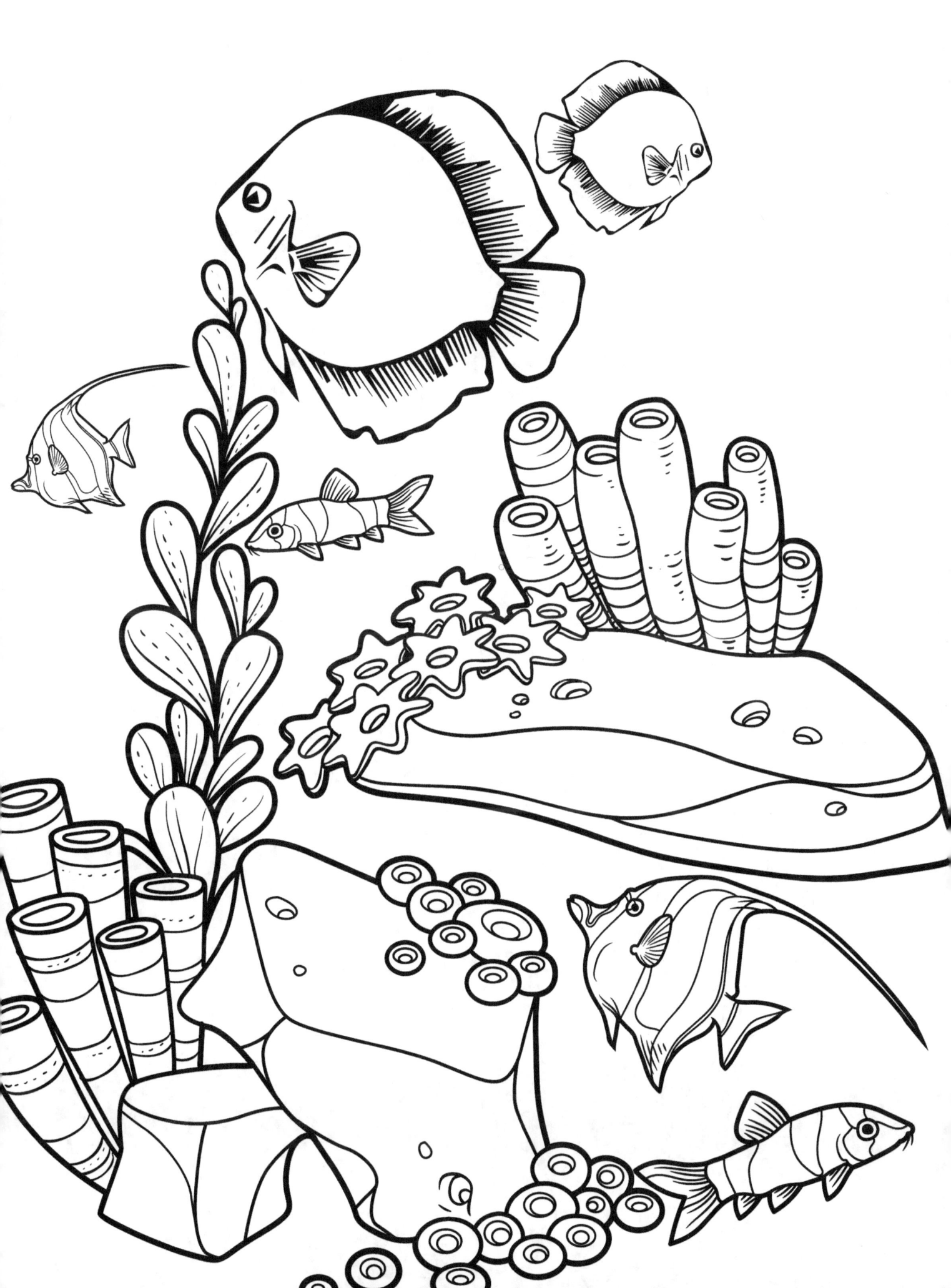

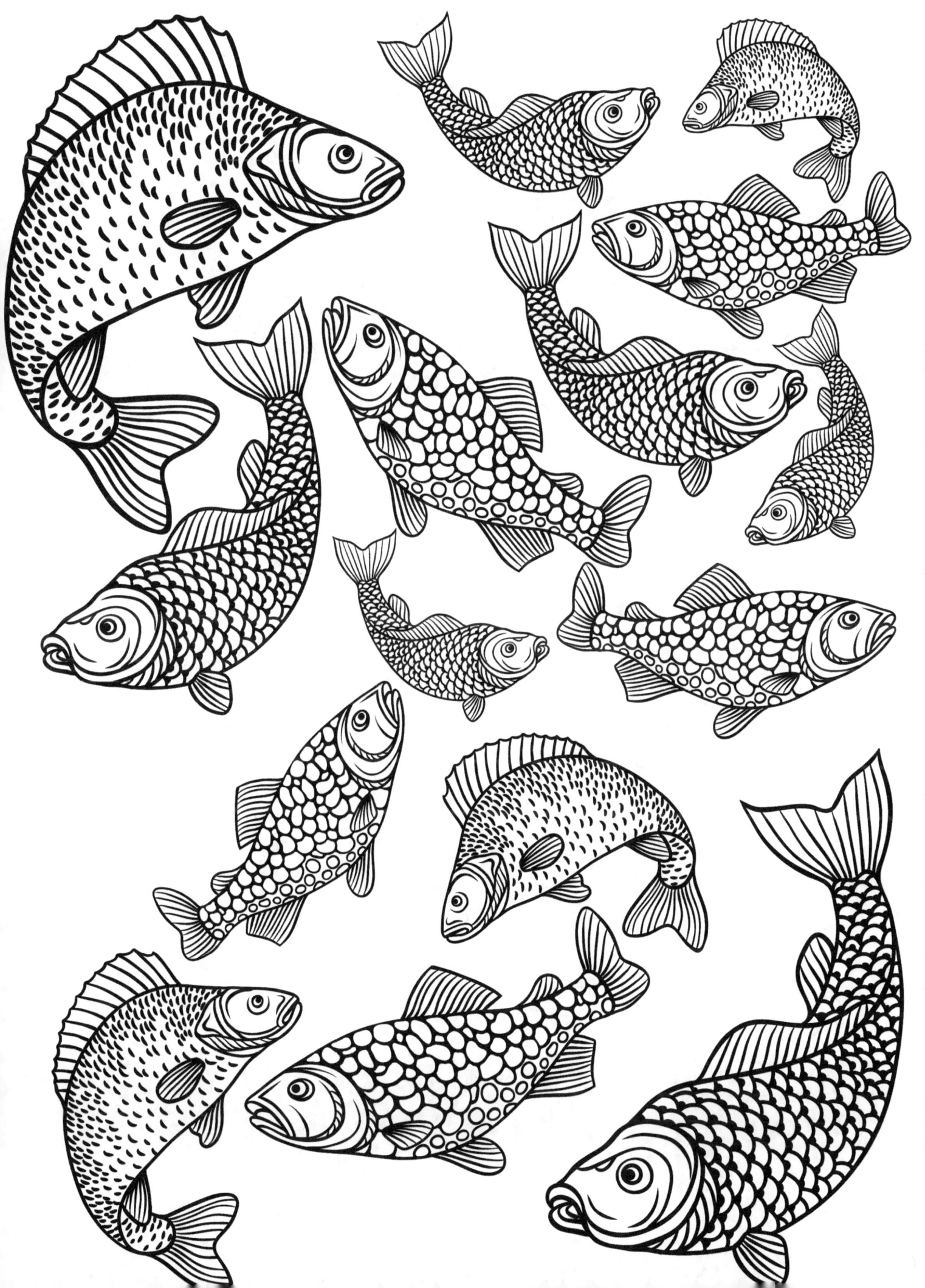

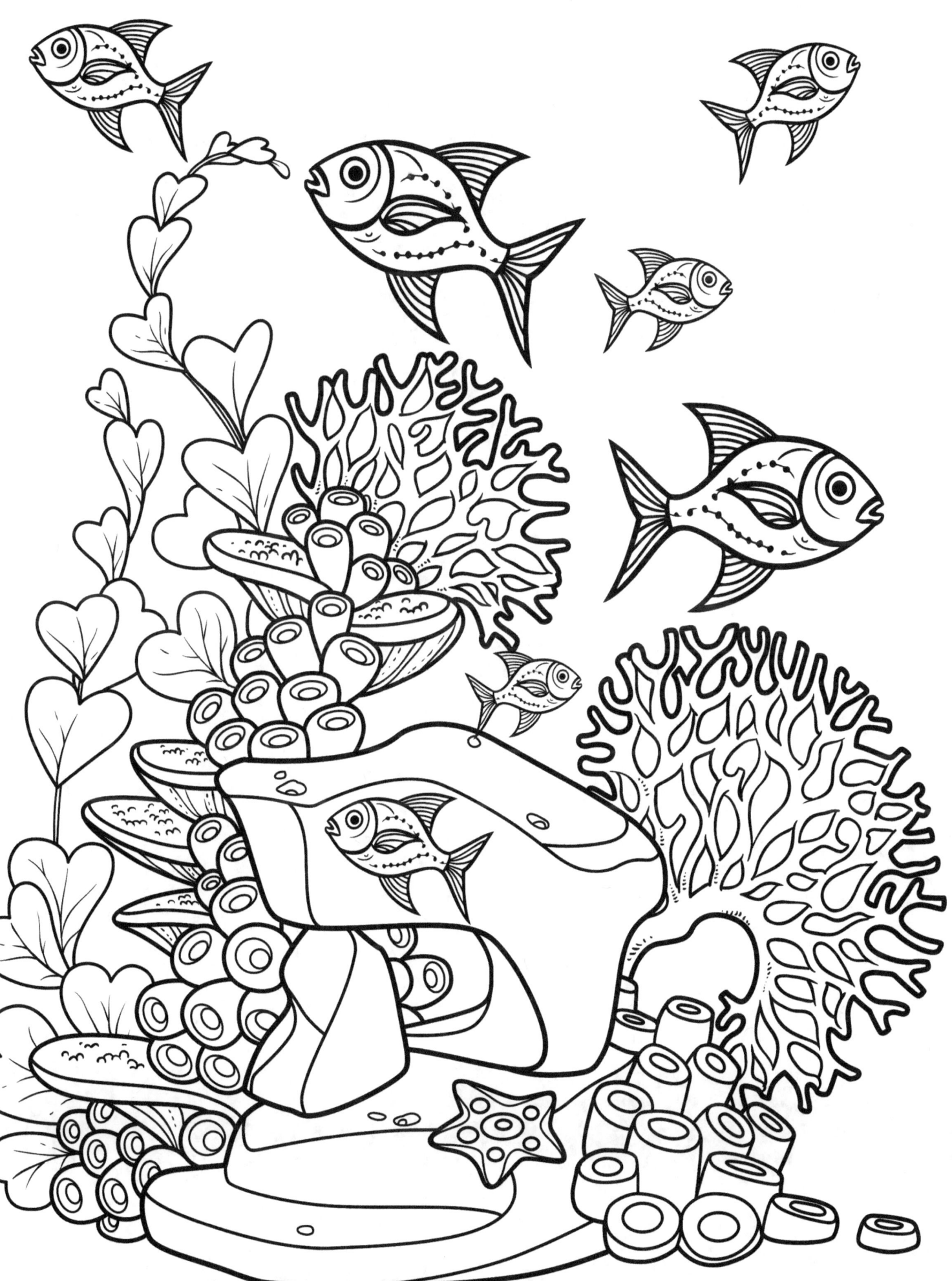

THANK YOU!

Thank you! For embarking on a fin-tastic coloring adventure with "Just Keep Coloring: A Fin-Tasticly Fishy Coloring Book"! I hope you enjoyed diving into the vibrant underwater world filled with charming fish and enchanting marine landscapes.

If you loved your coloring experience, I would greatly appreciate it if you could take a moment to leave a review of the book on Amazon. Your feedback helps me improve and ensures that other fish enthusiasts can discover the joy of coloring with my books.

To leave a review on Amazon, simply visit the product page for "Just Keep Coloring" and share your thoughts. Your support means the world to me!

Looking for more coloring fun? Check out some of my other titles available on Amazon:

- Bookish Blooms: A Cactus and Succulent Adult Coloring Book

- Color the Cosmos, A Space and Sci-Fi Adult Coloring

- Gnomes! A Coloring Book for All!

Explore these titles and discover even more coloring escapades that will spark your imagination and soothe your soul.

Once again, thank you for choosing "Just Keep Coloring: A Fin-Tasticly Fishy Coloring Book." Happy coloring!

Warm regards, Eve Jones

www.ingramcontent.com/pod-product-compliance
Lightning Source LLC
Chambersburg PA
CBHW062123220526
45471CB00010B/3850